**Rural development and
women in Africa**

Rural development and women in Africa

International Labour Office   Geneva

ISBN 92-2-103633-2

First published 1984
Second impression 1986

HQ
1240.5
,A35
R87
1986   /53,247

Printed in Switzerland   VAU

The World Employment Conference in June 1976 noted that in many developing countries women are particularly disadvantaged in respect of employment, poverty, education, training and status. Concerning rural women, the Conference recommended that measures be taken to relieve their work burden and drudgery by improving working and living conditions, as well as by providing more resources for investment. More recently, in November/December 1979, the ILO's Advisory Committee on Rural Development urged the ILO to continue and extend its work concerning women in rural development, with a special focus on women in the disadvantaged groups.

Within the International Labour Office, the Programme on Rural Women constitutes one of the ILO's attempts to translate these recommendations into action. In view of the inadequate research done on employment patterns and labour processes, poverty and organisations of rural women, the main focus of the Programme has been on studies and field research subcontracted to experts in the Third World. The general approach of the Programme is to move gradually from a substantial conceptual and information base to the dissemination and exchange of information and insights through seminars and workshops, followed by the planning and implementation of technical co-operation projects to assist the poorest strata among rural women, in close consultation, where possible, with rural women's own organisations.

Under the auspices of this Programme, and in co-operation with the Association of African Women for Research and Development (AAWORD), representatives of government, workers' and employers' organisations, donor countries, international organisations and researchers met in Dakar, Senegal, between 15 and 19 June 1981, to debate priority issues and suggest policy guide-lines for policy-makers and planners to take action to improve the living and working conditions of rural women in Africa. This report presents the views of participants, with whom the ILO is not necessarily in agreement. A list of participants is appended.

The ILO Tripartite African Regional Seminar on Rural Development and Women and the case studies which were prepared for it by
African women members of AAWORD were financed by the Federal Republic
of Germany, as part of an ILO-implemented inter-regional project.
Similar seminars were held in Asia and Latin America.

The Seminar took place on the premises kindly provided by the
African Institute for Economic Development and Planning (IDEP), who
also provided interpretation services.   It was hosted by the
Secrétariat d'Etat à la Promotion Humaine, Government of Senegal.

The themes which emerged from the research undertaken in Africa
included: food production and processing; commercialisation and
modernisation of agriculture; migration; organisation and policy
implications.   There were particular debates on: the national and
international context of rural development and the limitations thus
imposed on narrow initiatives and projects; approaches to developing
and introducing improved methods and tools to assist women in their
productive work in food processing; patterns, causes and the impact
on women of migration and resettlement; income-generating projects
for women; and strategies for promoting change.   The conclusions
were unanimously adopted by the participants, indicating priorities
in the areas of research and data collection, food production, rural
modernisation, migration and organisation.

This Seminar had its origins back in 1978 when the ILO in
Geneva brought together a number of experts engaged in research on
rural development and women in the Third World.   Some AAWORD members
were present, who felt that such a project could help them in their
ongoing research, stock-taking, and identifying areas needing more
effort and attention.   This Seminar was also enriched by the active
participation of various units in the ILO concerned with women and
development in Africa.   In addition to the Rural Employment
Policies Branch, which organised this Seminar, participants came
from the Employment and Technology Branch, the Southern African Team
for Employment Promotion, the Jobs and Skills Programme for Africa
and the ILO Regional Office for Africa, and a joint ILO/ECA
regional project within the African Research and Training Centre.
for Women.

The technical input from all of these experts, mingled with the valuable knowledge and experience brought by government, worker and employer representatives from many African countries, and representatives of FAO, UNESCO, the World Bank, the Federal Republic of Germany, the Netherlands and the United States, all combined to allow a substantial review of key issues relevant to rural development and women in Africa.   It is our hope that this report will enable the benefits of that valuable debate to reach many more people concerned with these issues, so that all of our efforts can have a much greater impact.

Dharam Ghai,
Chief,
Rural Employment Policies Branch.

TABLE OF CONTENTS

    * French language original.

* French language original.

PART I

PROCEEDINGS OF THE SEMINAR

INTRODUCTION

Rural development in Africa is inconceivable without the active participation of women.   They already provide a major part of the labour power and are involved in all sectors.   Yet it is quite clear that women's interests and needs are not always taken into account, nor is the most effective use made of women's capabilities.

With a view toward providing guidelines and principles for policy-makers and planners and ways of action to be undertaken at different levels, representatives of African governments, workers' and employers' organisations, international and non-governmental organisations and researchers met for five days in June 1981.   Faced with extensive research on the actual situation of rural women and development in a number of African countries (see Part II), the debate led to conclusions about rural development priorities in Africa (see Chapter 8).

They called for a reconsideration of rural development strategies, which must take account of the role of women in rural production and distribution in order to simultaneously ameliorate the working and living conditions of rural women and raise their productivity.   One of the steps in accomplishing this is a re-examination of the concepts and assumptions that presently underlie data collection and analysis, including "household", "housework", "work", "employment" and "farmer".

In order to improve the ability of African countries to meet their food needs, women have to be recognised as cultivators and given equitable access to land, credit, extension services and improved tools as well as to co-operatives and other rural workers' organisations.

This report summarises the debates that led participants to these conclusions (Part I, prepared by Martha Loutfi) and also presents summarised versions of the background papers (Part II, prepared by Elizabeth Eisold and edited by Teresa Mesa)

The opening session of the Seminar was addressed by Mr. Godonou Dossou and Ms. Martha Loutfi of the ILO, Ms. Cornelia Richter of the Federal Republic of Germany, and Mrs. Seynabou N'Dao of the Government of Senegal, who inaugurated the Seminar.

Godonou Dossou, then Deputy Director of the ILO Office in
Dakar, welcomed the participants and thanked the host Government
(in particular, the Secrétariat d'Etat à la Promotion Humaine),
the donor (the Federal Republic of Germany) and IDEP (the African
Institute for Economic Development and Planning) where the Seminar
was being held.   He noted that the results of the debate on food
production, commercialisation and modernisation of agriculture,
migration and grass root organisations of women were awaited with
great interest.   The attempts at improvement in conditions of
rural life could not be effective without taking account of the
evident economic roles of women.   Rural women produce, process,
transport and sell, being thus complete economic agents assuring
the essential functions from the field to market place.   One must
give dignity and confidence, however, to rural women, recognising
their force for development.

Martha Loutfi informed the participants that this Seminar was
one of three regional seminars taking place on Rural Development and
Women : one in Asia took place in April 1981; and the Latin American
one was scheduled two months hence.

As she explained, in a fundamental sense, this was not really
a seminar about women: it was a seminar about development,
especially rural development.   Production of food and provision of
fuel and water, for example, are basic problems of development.   But
they are also, typically, women's problems.   Attention to women's
problems, therefore, contributes to progress in national and
regional development.

Cornelia Richter offered some remarks concerning the promotion
of women in development policy of the Federal Republic of Germany.
She was very glad to be presenting them in the year 1981 and not
ten years earlier, as the past decade has been characterised by
conceptual development in development policy.   She focused on three
questions: What have been the reasons for the promotion of women in
German development policy?   What was the situation of women at the
moment in that development policy concerning the promotion of women?
What are the perspectives for further promotion of women?

Concerning the first question: The general answer must be
that the international discussion has given many impulses to national
policy in the Federal Republic of Germany, and in particular, three
new subjects have contributed to a new concept of development policy.

One was the discussion about the "target groups" as a result of losing the illusion that the "trickle down" to the poor was effective. Among these target groups, women have become one special target group, besides small peasants and the landless labourers. A second one was the discussion about basic needs, due to the fact that it was more important to tackle mass poverty than to promote large-scale projects. The new slogan was "not millions of projects but projects for millions of people". The third theme which also influenced the promotion of women and the conceptual design of policy was the discussion about rural development.

Concerning the second question, on the situation in 1981 in development policy of the Federal Republic of Germany, she thought that the international discussion in the above-mentioned fields had improved the awareness about women's key roles in development. Although one could say that there was much more awareness than ten years earlier, yet we were still at the very beginning. There was still a lack of knowledge about the importance of women's roles for project effectiveness and there were still many psychological problems also in the Federal Republic which constrained the promotion of women. Most of those responsible in administration, including her own, were men and normally they do not approach the problems like a woman. Another psychological factor seemed to be the fear of many men that the promotion of women was the policy of some radical feminists. The feminist movement has often been discriminated against in Europe, so sometimes when these problems were intermingled it hindered the promotion of women in developing countries. Nevertheless, some progress had been made in the past year in different dimensions. Some facts seemed worth mentioning.

Since February 1978 the Ministry has included in all its intergovernmental negotiations a Memorandum expressing the basic willingness of the federal Government to give increasing support to projects relevant to women. The reaction of the partner countries has moved from serious reservations to strong support. Numerous requests received for projects especially designed to help women from our partner countries in Africa, Asia and Latin America were certainly inspired by this Memorandum, which was a first step in connection with many other endeavours within the federal Government system of development co-operation, based upon requests from the partner countries. Another step was in project identification, where special missions have proved useful when it comes to including women in more development activities. In many countries the results of such missions were promotion of new or complementary

measures relevant to women within the ongoing projects (including
the Gambia, Ghana, Honduras, Indonesia, Mali, Mauritania, Peru,
Togo, Yemen and Zambia.   Another fact mentioned was a special
government fund - very small but a first beginning.   About
4.5 million Deutschmarks were set aside for the purpose of promoting
women in developing countries.   Another step was the preparation of
project appraisal criteria in order to ensure that the interests of
women were taken into account at an early stage of planning in as
many projects as possible.   And additions were made to the appraisal
guidelines on technical co-operation, which also contained details
on, for example, the labour distribution between men and women in
purchasing, production and marketing.   The aim of this was to try
to ensure that women benefit from development aid or at least are not
put at a disadvantage.   Within the scope of financial co-operation
too, the guidelines on agriculture, drinking water supply and
development banks were reviewed for their relevance to women.   And
in 1978 and 1979, projects in the field of food aid and food security
were analysed with respect to their relevance to women.   A catalogue
of questions was worked out for the future examination of the impact
of food-aid projects on women.   And another important step
involved research.   There was still a great lack of knowledge about
these problems, so they carried out country-related research projects
and worked out guidelines for the appraisal of projects aimed at
women.

Coming to the perspectives, she said that the Federal Republic
of Germany was still at the very beginning in its promotion policy.
But there was a lot of goodwill in the administration with respect to
learning more facts about the situation in developing countries and
that is why she was looking forward to this Seminar.   It was an
opportunity to learn new facts and go back with a new awareness
about the problems in Africa.

Mrs. Seynabou N'Dao stated that it was a privilege and
pleasure to open this tripartite Seminar on Rural Development and
Women, on behalf of the Secrétaire d'Etat à la Promotion Humaine.

The theme of the Seminar could not have been more appropriate,
in her view, at the moment when the Third World was determined to
make progress in all areas and when women were becoming more
confident and organising themselves, taking an increasingly
important role in the development process.   An examination of
rural reality revealed that in the Third World, not only women but

entire families were living in a state of total need.   Among these
millions of underprivileged people, many African women suffered
from a particular handicap because the possibilities for progress
were normally reserved for men.   The colonisers rarely recognised
the economic role of women and they encouraged men to undertake
cash crop production (e.g. cocoa, cotton, groundnuts, sugar cane)
needed by the industrial West.   Women had responsibility for home
and family as well as participating in production.   However, until
the recent past, programmes for African women seldom recognised
their role as producers even though they made an essential contribution to rural development, especially in agriculture, animal
husbandry, and fruit, vegetable and fish processing, etc.   This
contribution was demonstrated in different ways under different
economic systems but it determined the satisfaction of food and
monetary needs of the family.   In many cases, the participation of
women in development projects in their regions has been judged
insufficient.   It was thus that one has seen women pushed out of
projects for production (and agricultural mechanisation) of crops
traditionally in their domaine, such as rice.   Technologies which
could transform food grains into edible products often replaced
women rather than assisting them.   The provision of water and
processing of food were tasks traditionally falling upon women.
Given difficult terrain, these tasks constituted heavy drudgery,
conditioning their work time and subjecting them to a fatigue
rendering them unable to do much else.

In order to ameliorate the working conditions of rural women,
it was necessary to organise and focus on economically viable
operations.   In this regard, the Département de la Promotion
Humaine had the mission to promote the development of rural and
urban communities devoted to these tasks and to work continuously
to encourage women to organise themselves in order to facilitate
the initiation of collective production and distribution and to
permit them to benefit from certain facilities such as credit.

Upon declaring her profound conviction that the results of the
debates and reflections in the Seminar would permit gains in the
participation of women in rural development, Mrs. N'Dao officially
inaugurated the Seminar.

The following record of debates and presentation of background
material demonstrate the extent and intensity of results obtained
during the Seminar.   The vast subject area covered during the

Seminar was not fully digested and synthesised before the closing, but considerable excitement and momentum had been generated.

A field visit was arranged to Joal-Fadiouth, where research had been undertaken among women engaged in fish processing to determine appropriate forms of assistance.   The participants were welcomed by the mayor, Mr. Emmanuel Diouf, who explained some local issues in that fishing village.   A co-operative among women engaged in fish processing had been created eight years before but was inactive, with the women working and marketing individually. As a result of the research and the visit, the ILO is supporting a project among the women, focusing on organisational development.

The Seminar was closed with some brief commentary by Martha Loutfi for the ILO, Essam Montasser (Director) for IDEP and Aissatou Sow Barry for the Secrétariat d'Etat à la Promotion Humaine.

Ms. Loutfi expressed the gratitude of the ILO to the Govern- ment of Senegal, and particularly the Secrétariat d'Etat à la Promotion Humaine for hosting the Seminar; to the Federal Republic of Germany, who supported the research and the Seminar; to IDEP, for hospitality and services rendered; to AAWORD, through which the ILO carried out research in various countries; and to the participants, coming from a large number of countries, representing governments, workers, employers and international organisations, for the various insights and experiences they shared during the few days of the Seminar, which should make efforts in pursuit of rural development and the amelioration of the condition of poor women in rural areas more effective.

She offered a few reflections.   The Rural Employment Policies Branch of the ILO, which sponsored this Seminar, was committed to the participation of the poor in rural development, and has been trying, both in research and in assistance projects, to minimise bureaucracy, decentralise and reach to the grass roots as far as possible.   Sometimes that effort has been more successful, sometimes less successful; the effort continues.   But there was a hope that the time would come - sooner rather than later - when more African organisations, voluntary agencies, trade unions, employers and planning ministries would take up the issues of rural development and women in a broader and more sustained way, so that all efforts could be mutually reinforcing.

During the Seminar a considerable amount of time was spent discussing "income-generating activities" and "projects" for women. That was necessary and constructive. But still, one could wonder why there was a tendency to consider "income generating projects" for women and "employment" for men? Only when one finds that the interest and needs of poor rural women are fully reflected in the national machineries and planning processes and one can move beyond relying on discrete projects, will progress surely have been made.

Mr. Montasser offered some concrete encouragement. Most participants knew that IDEP has always in the past stood by progressive ideas and causes. In fact, quite often they have participated in the conceptualisation and initiation of such ideas, last but not least "collective self-reliance". He expressed support for the cause of women in development believing strongly that there can be no achievement of the goals of development in Africa without major upheavals in the women's sector.

In the past, economists have spoken mainly about "labour" in development as a homogeneous group. But recent literature on women pointed out clearly that there are some non-competing groups within the labour force and among these non-competing groups are women, who constitute about 50 per cent of the adult population. This situation has historical, social, cultural and economic reasons, which go back a long, long time. Much of the work that has been recently initiated, including this Seminar, has been crystalising and pointing out those barriers which made women into non-competing groups within the labour force. Furthermore, it has been shedding much light on how we could eliminate these barriers - because it is only through the elimination of these barriers (whether legal, social or other), that women would become a homogeneous part of the labour force and be unshackled and accordingly, could contribute the maximum to development. For this progress he was grateful.

It had been arranged and agreed upon that in the future, IDEP would play a major role in the structuring and programming of an African regional programme under the auspices of the Lagos Plan of Action (referring to the economic summit that took place in Lagos), he reported. Since IDEP was going to be playing a major role in this, he invited participants - individuals and institutions - to contribute to IDEP's efforts and to collaborate in these areas. He invited guidance on how to develop and on what should be in a strategy

for the women's sector as a sector in the African economy as a whole.
IDEP would take this strategy and integrate it in an overall
strategy and development pattern for Africa, guaranteeing consistency.
By doing this, IDEP would expose participants' ideas, and bring them
further forward towards actual implementation. The first initial step
towards planting an idea is wonderful, to think of it, study it,
crystallise it; but the next step, which is probably the hardest,
is to move it towards implementation, bringing it closer to the
decision-making process, programmes and plans for implementation.
The Lagos Plan of Action was an important inroad to this process.
IDEP is going to be playing a role in it and welcomes any contributions and collaboration from individuals and institutions. Then
IDEP could integrate ideas into the over-all strategy of the region
and then bring them closer to implementation.

In closing the Seminar, Mrs. Barry thanked the ILO for its happy
initiative to organise the Seminar on Rural Development and Women,
the Federal Republic of Germany for its support, IDEP for welcoming
the Seminar on its premises, participants for their constructive
contributions to debates, AAWORD for their participation in the
Seminar, and the interpreters for enabling the linguistic barriers
to be transcended. And she expressed the hope that the conclusions
thus reached in Dakar would have a real impact on the living and
working conditions of rural women in the countries to which each
would return.

Chapter 1

AN OVERVIEW

Presentation: Zenebeworke Tadesse

In the past, most discussions and policy decisions concerning agricultural production omitted any serious consideration of women's role in agriculture. Moving towards a healthy corrective, the last decade was marked by the emergence of empirical and theoretical documentation of women's multiple roles in production and reproduction. Within these studies, the issue of undernumeration of women's work in existing census data resulting from faulty conceptual categories in forming data collection, women's role in food production and women's lack of access to strategic resources seem to have received priority in narrowing the existing knowledge gap.

In recent years, of particular importance to the debate on women's roles has been the need to conceptualise the significance of the sexual division of labour. This in turn has generated initial inquiries: what are the tasks and responsibilities of women, men and children at the farm level, in the household and in the community? Do these tasks and responsibilities change over time? How does society value each task?

In order to supplement the gap in pre-existing knowledge, concern with women's roles has resulted in a descriptive addition of labour flow data by sex and an exclusive focus on women's roles, but without providing an analysis of the overall determinants of agricultural transformation and the resultant changes and/or continuity of the pre-existing sexual division of labour. As a result, contrary to well-meant intentions, policies drawn from such studies have in many instances just increased women's workload. To avoid past mistakes, future discussions have not only to include women but examine the reasons why women's work was and still continues to be devalued. (See Chapter I, Part II.)

Persistent myths about African agriculture

Many myths still persist, in spite of the progress.

1. The concept "farmer" denotes only men and implies that at best women only assist in agricultural production: this myth has great implications for the allocation of resources and training to women in agriculture.

2.   Women do not participate in cash crop production: the fact is
they participate as an unremunerated familial labour force and
seasonal workers on plantations.   It is not that they do not
participate, but they do not control the income from cash crop
production.

3.   Modernisation and development are neutral and inherently
beneficial processes: the fact is that the primary aim of these
programmes is producing surplus to sell to the international or
urban markets and entails a variety of technical inputs which come
as a package.   Changes are both class and sex specific in that they
are mainly aimed at reaching "progressive farmers" who are often
assumed to be only men with larger assets.

4.   Modernisation programmes are based on a definition of the
"household" that assumes convergent interests where benefits are
shared equally by all members: there is a need to re-examine the
concept of household, since the literature now shows that the impact
of programmes and policies differs according to sex.

5.   Housework is a simple activity separate from production and
concerned with immediate household consumption: yet much is aimed
at the market.   But women's participation in production is not
sufficient to improve women's condition.

    The last decade has generated an awareness that, contrary to
old assumptions, African women constitute a crucial sector of the
agriculture labour force.   This awareness is the key to understanding one major cause of rural poverty as well as the potential
and limits of agricultural development in Africa.   Furthermore,
agriculture is the main form of production in Africa, where on
the average 70 per cent of the population is employed and
over 80 per cent of the cash earnings are generated.   Therefore to
understand the role of rural women, we have to first look at the
determinants of agricultural production and the division of labour
by sex.   Similarly, to understand changes in agricultural production
and household allocation of labour, we have to understand the
changing demands of the world economy.

    This brings forth some methodological imperatives:

    We cannot begin to talk about agricultural production in
Africa without locating it within the world economy and the changing
nature of the international division of labour.   Secondly, we
cannot discuss agricultural production without examining the

specific nature of the sexual division of labour within the household and the changes in the household allocation of labour brought
about by the changes in the international division of labour.

African agriculture and the
world economy

With the exception of the mining enclaves, Africa was primarily
incorporated into the world economy as a region for the production
of agricultural raw materials.   Since the 1950s, a period coinciding
with the beginning of independence for most African countries, Africa
like most other Third World areas, has also become a site for
import substitution industrialisation.

In turn, this form of industrialisation has resulted in the
growth of urban centres, with an ever increasing population divorced
from agriculture, and in the further integration of Africa into the
world economy, as a purchaser of technology and commodities necessary
for urban living.

Once integrated, the developments in Africa have been subject
to the changing demands of the global accumulation process.   The
changing demands of the world market have had a tremendous impact on
agricultural production, the relations of production and reproduction.
The most significant change in agriculture is the growth of commercial
agriculture, where priority in resource allocation is given to the
production of cash crops for the export and urban markets.   For most
of Africa, agricultural exports account for the major share of foreign
exchange earnings.   Agricultural production is constantly subject to
the vagaries of the world market prices and demand where in recent
years the terms of trade for primary producers have gone from bad to
worse.   This in turn has an impact on the rural-urban terms of trade
where a variety of policies have attempted to either constantly reduce
and/or freeze grain prices in spite of rising costs of imported agricultural inputs and other commodities.

Low grain prices and high cost of farm inputs force rural households to intensify cash crop production and the labour process within
the household,and to participate in the labour market and other forms
of income-generating activities.   Furthermore, investment in
industrial production is premised on payment of relatively low wages
to industrial workers.   In turn, low wages presuppose keeping food
prices relatively low in addition to non-wage supplements that are
provided by non-wage members of the workers' household, i.e. mostly
women and children.

In sum, the penetration of capital in every aspect of rural
life where cash has become a necessity forces the rural population
into intensifying cash crop production to the detriment of food
production.   The most fertile lands and the major aspect of institutional support and agricultural budget are set aside for the
development of export crops, drawing resources away from the
subsistence sector, and leading to a growing class differentiation.
Local production has not been able to meet the growing local demand
for agricultural products.

In other words the deteriorating terms of trade for primary
producers at the global level and the rising cost of technology
that African countries have to import, together with the emergence
of new class structures, have generated a process where cash crop
production for export is given a priority at the cost of sacrificing
self-sufficiency in food production.   Almost all African countries
have been forced to import food products in addition to many other
commodities.   Women from poor households as principal providers of
food to the household are the most negatively affected members of
rural Africa.   Against all these odds, they continue to meet their
primary obligations.

Women and food production

The sexual division of labour in food production is both task
and crop specific.   The predominant role of women in food production
is widely documented: they provide 70 per cent of the labour in
food production and are solely responsible for food processing.
Women carry out the time-consuming and numerous tasks subsumed under
the categories of food processing, preparation and storage.   These
are not generally seen as agricultural work, yet many food crops are
neither saleable nor edible without that processing.

In almost all cases women are responsible for provisioning
almost all food consumption needs in the family.   Although women
had decision-making power concerning food production, the significance
of this power has been eroded by the penetration of capital into the
rural areas resulting in the increased importance of cash crop
production, the diversion of better, more convenient land to those
crops and changing food habits where rural households are forced to
buy part of their food, etc.   As a result, women are forced to sell
more than the surplus, spend time on their husband's cash crops, and
engage in a variety of income-generating activities in order to meet

their familial obligations, which means that women's roles are multiplying, contributing to low productivity.

The importance given to cash crop production has been accompanied by a variety of "modernising schemes" and development programmes which have all transformed the value of ownership and control of land, methods of production and division of labour by sex. The most significant of these changes is the process of social differentiation set in motion by the creation of the markets for land and labour. Very few women can afford to buy land, and the land they have access to is generally inferior land. Yet they have to contribute their labour on the land of others, e.g. on plantations and for cash crops. There is a need to look at agricultural modernisation schemes, especially "integrated rural development" schemes, because they have new effects on rural households.

Agricultural modernisation

The pattern of agricultural development involves a variety of technical and other innovations, new irrigation schemes, cash cropping, use of tractors, integrated rural development programmes, introduction of land saving biological and chemical technology (e.g. HYV and fertilisers).

Agricultural modernisation alters cropping patterns and necessitates the allocation of new inputs and more labour. Most studies show that these schemes for the most part have tended to increase women's workload, reduce their decision-making power and strengthen their traditional obligation to feed the household. Women's labour increases disproportionately because they still have to carry household maintenance and child care in addition to their role in food production and the new forms of production.

Generally, development projects, no matter how "integrated", do not include labour-saving devices for women, which helps to explain why women cannot fulfil all that is expected of them in these projects.

Modernisation necessitates changes in land tenure, new agricultural skills and co-operative marketing. Projects in these areas are generally premised on the household as a unit of convergent interests where the costs and benefits of the schemes will be evenly shared by both sexes. There is a need for an evaluation of the labour process and sexual division of labour to bring the reality to light.

Disappearance of communal land tenure dispossesses women of land and recognising men as the new owners of land decreases women's control over productive resources. Credits and loans are less readily available to women, as they are made against land titles or made through co-operative societies of which men are mainly members. Also agricultural extension services are unequally channelled to men and women. In most cases, agricultural extension services focus on men as the only target group and identification of "improved farmers" is both sex and class biased. Schemes aimed at the "progressive" farmer exclude not only women but also many of the poor. This bias is particularly damaging in areas of large-scale male migration, where there should be no doubt as to who the farmers are, as in southern Africa and parts of East and West Africa. In cases where males migrate, tasks traditionally regarded as theirs are necessarily taken over by women, yet extension services are not available to them.

In addition, women need the chance to benefit collectively. The form of organisation can vary however, and many present women's organisations cater only to a subset of urban women.

Discussion

Participants focused on the general issue of what was the appropriate level at which to seek change - global, regional, national, rural, class, household, etc. Some argued that a global approach was necessary, because only then can one understand the larger, interlinked processes. The task was no longer to take an inventory of "women's tasks" it was argued, but to sensitise and conscientise people. This required attention to the underlying concepts and theories. Past approaches had too often been symptomatic, without looking at the context and the global picture. Talk about lack of data, specific technologies, and sectoral issues has tended to divert attention from the larger questions. Unless the processes of development, the changes which have been occurring and the polarisation are examined, one cannot understand what is happening. The "integration of women in development" has become a cliché with an unclear meaning. Yet, it was argued, these discussions could lead toward the development of concrete proposals, once deeper understanding was achieved.

One should only look at rural development in the context of national and international strategies, it was stated. Only then could one understand, for example, why West Africa had become an

area of male migration, and why peanut production in Senegal
increasingly depended on female and immigrant labour.   Women were
drawn progressively into more agricultural work while continuing
their domestic tasks, a process which could not be analysed in
isolation.   It was, inter alia, linked to overall food systems.

On the issue of class vs. sex differentiation, participants
generally agreed that most women are exploited, without denying the
fact that some men are also.   Some men exploit both other men as
well as women.   Some men as well as women are marginalised by the
development process.   Although some men may be limited in their
authority by chiefs and others above them, men benefit from patriarchal structures within the household and control of women's labour.
One should not lose sight of double discrimination, by sex as well
as class, it was argued.   When the household becomes worse off,
much more of the burden tends to fall on women, who have to ensure
the family's food and carry out the most burdensome tasks.   Men and
women in rural households did not start out as equal, and patriarchal
structures and authorities have given more resources to men, so the
inequality increases.   And more and more women are solely responsible for their families' survival.   The sexual division of labour
interacted with the changing structures in rural areas in a way that
has worked to the detriment of women.

With most participants convinced of the problem, the issues of
specific actions to change the attitudes of others and of the value
of special projects for women were raised.

One participant still felt that there is some special work more
suited to women, and that this was the justification of separate
projects for women along with integrated projects.   But there was a
strong reaction against this view as being patronising.   Another
point raised was the risk of taking too narrow an economic view,
neglecting the broader questions of women's status and legal position, including access to credit.

Reasons for the often inadequate effectiveness of women's
projects were queried, along with the political, economic and
social prerequisites for integration of women in the development
process.   But another participant argued that women have not really
been left out.   Projects have tended to be ineffective because
of their assumption that women were not involved, where in fact
work was expected of women.   In this way, many projects ended up
being unsuccessful, while increasing women's work burden and
worsening their condition.

The use of the concepts of "work" and "employment" was raised. The distinction between unpaid and paid work underlay the problem being discussed, it was argued. The increasing importance of and need for cash income devalued unpaid work; yet its importance remained basic. As a result, it was not obvious what the most appropriate intervention point was. If the persistence of unpaid work was due to national strategies and the international economy, then the implications for those who seek improvement were different than they would be if the problem were inside the household. It was also important to distinguish the level where decisions were made when considering work and employment, it was added. And the distinctions were not fixed but mutable, with what was work vs. non-work a decade ago different from what it was now.

In sum, the presentation and discussion covered a wide range of conceptual, theoretical and strategic questions. The broader framework was thus aired before going on to a more specific consideration of information, approaches and policies.

Chapter 2

FOOD PRODUCTION AND PROCESSING
AND TECHNOLOGICAL INTERVENTION

Presentation: Yvette Stevens and Eugenia Date-Bah

Rural women are responsible for multiple labour-intensive and
time-consuming chores both inside and outside of their household.
On a daily basis, women's activities include "domestic" chores such
as cooking, fetching water and fuel, household maintenance and
child care.   In addition, rural women are responsible for food
cultivation, food preservation and storage.   Each task in turn
involves a series of other sub (labour) processes.   Furthermore,
these various tasks are laborious, time-consuming and wasteful
because of the rudimentary tools that women use, lack of institutional support and infrastructural problems such as the need to
fetch water and fuel from long distances.   Much of this is, or
should be, obvious.   Therefore, technological interventions that
would reduce work burdens can make an important contribution to
solving rural women's problems.   One needs to look at the points
of intervention and the means.   The focus here is not on advanced
technologies, but on improved technologies, tools and techniques
which would enable rural women to increase output and income and
remove some health hazards involved with traditional tools and
methods. (See Chapters 3 and 4, Part II).

Cultivation

Women plant, weed, harvest and carry the produce home from the
farms.   The introduction of cash cropping has meant that women have
less help from men who are now fully engaged in cash cropping and
women too have to work on the cash crop in addition to their subsistence food production tasks.   Women's productivity is low
because of the small size of their farms; the considerable distance
of the farms from the village; the land tenure system which discriminates against women in the allocation of land for farming;
the rudimentary tools that women work with; lack of access to
credit; lack of agricultural extension inputs; and the numerous
other chores that women have to perform in addition to food crop
farming.   Often the only equipment used is a tractor - for
ploughing, a male task.

Food processing

Women typically are solely responsible for food processing both for home consumption and sale.

Food processing entails tasks such as threshing, drying, winnowing, peeling, grating, sieving, pounding, etc. Since these tasks are performed with traditional tools and techniques, they tend to be tedious and time-consuming in addition to raising the risk of contamination and other forms of wastage. And some "improvements" or innovations involve an increase in that burden, for example, women rejected high yielding maize because it was difficult to process. Appropriate mills, stoves for smoking and palm oil presses, for example, do exist, although they may also involve problems for women in obtaining fuel, in addition to the basic obstacles they face in gaining access to new technologies.

Food preservation

Women are also responsible for food preservation. A predominant example is that of fish smoking and drying. They constitute another set of time-consuming tasks. The time and drudgery involved in performing these various tasks can be greatly reduced through the introduction of appropriate technology. For example, there are certainly more economical ways of drying food than laying it on the ground - e.g. solar dryers, which can save time and energy while producing a better product.

In recent years, concern with the plight of rural women has generated a search for appropriate technology that would increase output and income while reducing the time and energy that is presently invested in the multiplicity of tasks that women have to perform. The introduction of such technology would entail non-capital-intensive tools which would be geared to improving skills and techniques of the rural population. In order to fulfil these objectives, consideration must be given at the outset to acceptance by rural women and the inter-related issue of a dissemination strategy.

Acceptance: Taking stock of socio-economic factors

Before technology is introduced, a number of socio-economic and cultural factors have to be assessed. The first set of variables to be taken into consideration have to do with economic viability and technical efficiency. Given the poverty level of the rural poor and particularly women among them, the technology to be introduced has to be very cheap. Some cost reduction methods can be cited such as use of locally-available power sources, materials and skills. All these factors will be reflected in the capital, operating, maintenance and repair costs of the equipment. Introduction (payment) is particularly difficult, however, with respect to technologies to assist tasks which do not produce a cash income.

The efficient use of the technology will depend on the time and labour required to produce a given unit of output because in rural areas these two are crucial considerations, as technology can reduce and/or increase both time and energy required to complete a given task. Efficiency will also depend on considerations such as the materials required for manufacture, the ease with which an item can be manufactured, the ease of repair and maintenance and the complexity of design. In addition to these issues of economic viability and technical efficiency, serious consideration should be given to socio-cultural norms and values of a given population.

In some cases, problems arise because the women are used to working as a group whereas the new technology requires individual work.

Women have also been known to reject some technology which was introduced without considering pre-existing beliefs, taboos, attitudes, etc. Some of these include:

- accustomed ways of using and manipulating the body in various positions to hold and use tools. For example, women usually sit while cooking. The introduction of a cooking stove which stands high on the ground and which was so designed in order to protect the food being cooked from dust seems to have been rejected in some cases because of the standing body-posture it required;

- similarly in all societies, some body positions are defined as indecent. Therefore, some technologies which have been introduced have been rejected because their manipulation required the adoption of a body position which was considered as improper in their social values. Examples include a pedal operated grinding machine which was disseminated in Central Africa but was rejected because women had to stand astride, a body posture considered indecent for women;

- rural women allocate specific time in the day to specific activities. For example, rural women in Africa cook the main meal of the day after returning from the farm around sunset. Without taking consideration of the time budget or

comfort of women, solar reflective cookers were introduced
which required cooking when the sun was still hot and cooking
outside the house.   Women rejected this technology because of
the time factor, because they cook inside the house, and because
of the evident inconvenience in tropical countries of cooking
outdoors when the sun is strongest.

Other cultural factors include taboos such as those surrounding
the fertility of a woman.   In Ghana, for example, women do not
touch a bullock, because they believe they would be rendered
infertile.

Additional considerations include taste, texture and colour of
a final product, which contribute to a rejection or acceptance of
rural food technologies.   For example, one model of a stove for
fish smoking was rejected because of the unaccustomed effect on the
final product.   A cheaper model, producing an end product similar
to the traditional one, was quickly accepted.

Finally, an important factor contributing to the rejection
and/or acceptance of technology is the learning or socialisation
process through which people have internalised certain patterns of
behaviour.   Depending on the age, level and educational exposure
of the person, acceptance of improved technologies may require a
process of resocialisation to a different pattern of behaviour.

Dissemination strategy

In order to reach rural women and create the conditions which
would facilitate acceptance and a long lasting use of technology,
the above considerations require a variety of generation of technological innovations and dissemination strategies.   In general,
technologies have to be tried out and demonstrated in rural areas,
and their introduction should constitute a package which includes
loans and perhaps assistance in forming organisations.

Research and development institutions should: involve the
prospective users when planning and developing unproved technologies;
use indigenous resources (e.g. local artisans) for maintenance and
repair of improved technologies; and use renewable energy sources
as a replacement for manual and human power as far as possible.

Dissemination strategies should also be based on realities of
rural areas.   There is therefore a need for research and development
institutions to: create dissemination centres in the rural areas,

which could serve as links between them and rural people; diffuse
innovations through traditional media, institutions and popular
groups among the rural population (e.g. songs were effective in
introducing insecticides, and popular itinerant, drama groups could
explain new technologies); and work through existing organisations
or help form multi-purpose co-operatives or other organisations that
would be able to reach and involve rural villages and make villagers
aware of a given technology as well as to make credit available for
the purchase of the technology (e.g. the Ghana Council of Women has

adopted such a policy). Many co-operatives have not worked due
to political factors, with people pressurised to join. That
is not to negate the importance of organisation, but one should
try to build on existing forms where possible.

Major constraints in the introduction of appropriate technology

Given the low income of the rural population, a major constraint is the relatively high cost of the innovations introduced.

As research and development institutions have limited finances,
limited vehicles, etc., their pilot and demonstration efforts reach
only a small minority. There is very little effort at follow up,
monitoring and evaluation of existing projects, a failure which
prevents the possibility of learning from success or failures.
Research and development institutions in the same country have no
co-ordinated research and innovation programmes, with a resulting
duplication of efforts, lack of communication and sharing
information.

In addition, any technical assessment of traditional
technologies has generally been restricted to a particular
productive process without taking into consideration the backward,
forward and horizontal linkages among several activities performed
within a farming household. Introduction of innovations that do
not take into consideration the integrated nature of personal and
household operations risks the danger of rejection or an increase
in the labour input expected of household members, particularly
women. Failure to see the integrated nature of production
processes has led to inappropriate dichotomies, such as perceiving
some tasks as strictly consumption and others as production, the

latter receiving a priority consideration in the introduction of
technology as they are seen as crucial to the national economy.
However, this approach is based on a misconception of rural work.
For example, water is often considered a consumption item where in
fact it is also crucial for part of agricultural production and
processing. Similarly, storage hardly ever receives any policy
attention whereas wastage of grains due to lack of proper storage
depletes the amount of food available.

Discussion

The discussion following the presentation posed some basic
questions, such as: How cheap is cheap?   How appropriate is
appropriate?   Appropriate for whom?   Who exactly benefits from
this "appropriate technology" and why is it now felt that Africa
needs appropriate technology?   Given the fact that the ideology
behind what is appropriate for Africa as well as the original design
and parts would be brought from external sources, what is the
implication for the balance of payments?   Contrary to conventional
assumptions, the rural population is not a homogeneous group.
Given this reality, who gets access to credit?   What are the
implications of technology being accessible only to certain strata
of the rural population?

It was pointed out that a meaningful discussion on policy
cannot be formulated without a serious consideration of the above
questions, the answer of which requires an examination of a country's
overall development strategy, the politics behind global transfer
of technology generated by accumulation of capital and accelerating
North-South polarisation and the process of social differentiation.

What may seem cheap to an urban male official may be impossibly
expensive to a poor rural woman given her very limited access to
resources.   This was particularly true when the work to be
assisted does not yield any income, it was argued.

It was stressed that the assumption that rural women do not
accept or are slow to accept innovation is a false assumption generated by an ideology of disdain for rural people; and it is a concrete
symptom of blaming the victim.   Given the precarious nature and
economic insecurity of the rural poor, women are cautious rather than
backward.   Once convinced of the usefulness of a given innovation,
rural women not only accept it but have often adapted and improved
the technique.

In summary, it is essential to take an integrated view - of a woman, society and broader processes.   One cannot look at technologies, particularly household technologies, in isolation. And one needs to build on the technological knowledge of the people who are to be helped.   In many cases, people can assist others - a transfer between "target groups".

Chapter 3

COMMERCIALISATION AND MODERNISATION
OF AGRICULTURE

Presentation: Aminata Traoré

Some lessons can be drawn from the study on the access of women
in the Ivory Coast to resources.   Land is the primary and most
important resource, the base for all other agricultural activities.
Integration of women in development cannot mean much if nothing is
done about women's access to land.

The Ivory Coast, in the international context, is a producer of
coffee and cacao.   Its two principal characteristics are plantations,
with a long history in some regions, and the massive intervention of
the State in the promotion of commercialisation.   There, as in other
countries, some land was taken over on the grounds that it was not
being utilised; often that was land necessarily left fallow. Within
the country there have been greater differences since 1946, with some
areas becoming furnishers of labour and others, producers of agricultural products for cash.

The study prepared by the presenter (see Chapter 5, Part II)
focuses on the region, Adioukrou, whose principal characteristics
are: the antiquity of palm oil production, dating from the
eighteenth century, which has permitted the population to develop
trade with the coast, without upsetting their social organisation;
the recent state intervention in this sector, according to the
"Palm Plan", an element of the policy of diversification of agricultural yields; and the very strong impact of this plan, in
particular in the manner in which it progressively pushed women
toward another sector - that of the intensive and hard production
of the traditional food, attiéké, made from cassava (or manioc).   It
is essential to understand the place and the importance of women in
this economic strategy in order to search for solutions to the
food problems.

There is a very big difference between the traditional and the
modern palm oil production.   In the latter, the peasants just
become furnishers of palm to the modern sector, and women are left
out.   Attiéké production and marketing are done by women, the latter
activity producing the greater profit.   Traditionally, cassava was
planted between oil palms; in the modern form of growing selected
oil palms, there is no room for cassava, which must be grown elsewhere.

The policy of the State has been "land to the tiller", but land was not given to women, even where they constituted an important proportion of agricultural labour. Women are rarely considered proprietors, but they can utilise land on their own if they have the means to clear it (which they generally do not have). Men tend to be considered proprietors partly because it is they who clear the land, giving it agricultural value.

Women's response to this problem - their intensive production of attiéké - suffers from a lack of commercial networks and technology. The State created a factory in order to avoid an eventual shortage of this food, but this solution has not created employment. Research institutes are working on simple and more appropriate technologies, a subject already initiated in the context of the studies on Ghana and Sierra Leone.

It has been emphasised that African States, increasingly condemned to spend an important part of their hard currency on the importation of cereals, are aware of the urgency in developing their food sectors. They have an interest in constructing local food systems, in which women have a preponderant role to play. But this perspective, which seems completely realistic, seems to be in contradiction with the economic analysis whereby the States and employers draw profit from the situation of women, who assure the reproduction of the labour force needed by the market, permitting the maintenance of low salaries for workers.

Presentation: Awa Thiongane

Land registration policy in Senegal has had an important impact on women. (See Chapter 6, Part II.) In origin, the land and agricultural reform were linked in the early 1970s with the objective of creating an adequate structure for participation of the rural population. Those administering it were not, however, trained to understand the spirit of the reform.

Women had no specific place in the reform of territorial administration. Some women in fact heard of it for the first time when we researchers came to ask them about its impact. Others reported that men went to meetings but did not inform them of the substance. At the time of the research there were only four women among 500 counsellors in the region, although women participate more than men in the elections for one-third of the counsellors.

Women's situation with respect to access to land differs from one ethnic group to another, but had not changed seven years after the reform was instituted. Women's access tended to be fragile, with husbands allotting them some and, in case of divorce, brothers being asked to share land on women's return to their village of origin.

The land reform included the innovation of producers' groupings - but they were for the men. Extension workers played a social role with respect to the women, strengthening their domestic roles rather than supporting them as producers, and not modifying the situation of women within the family. There were some groups of women for food processing - milling, dehusking, etc. But the women had considerable difficulties with storage and marketing, and revenue was diverted to prestige expenditure for local administration instead, e.g., for generators.

Women continue to have difficulty in gaining access to the main means of production - land - or to co-operatives, which are the source of important inputs, e.g. seeds. Women cannot become direct members of the co-operative, and are allocated fewer inputs for their land. The process of research led to informing women about their rights - but only 12 villages were affected, and many more need to be reached.

Producers' groups among women could be a start, but they would still have limited access to land and inputs. The women did not see the existing groups as a potential source of power, and they were disappointed with results obtained. For example, researchers found mills which had been broken for years.

The woman is clearly present in the modernisation process, but she is not clearly perceived and her condition has not improved.

Discussion

Is it welfare of women in rural areas that is the objective, or is it employment for them, it was queried. Do we really want women to be allocated land separately from their husbands? Guidance was sought from the ILO; but it was made clear that the purpose of the Seminar was for the participants to debate and provide guidance on priorities, not for the ILO to provide answers to such questions. Divergence of opinion based on divergent experiences and interests was to be expected.

Along with governments and others, however, the ILO is concerned with the insufficiency of food. For food production, the producers - largely women - have to have access to land. In the Ivory Coast, for example, there is room for manoeuvre. The bottleneck is women's lack of access to male labour to clear the land; migrant labour is available but they cannot afford it.

Women are not only marginalised with respect to land, but also with respect to products they produce - the example already given of traders in urban areas obtaining a disproportionate share of the gain from attiéké.

This focus on commercialisation and other processes was seen as complementary to the previous discussion on specific technologies and their dissemination. For technologies, one is talking about investment and credit, for which land rights and legal status are critical. Thus it is essential to analyse various processes at different levels, including the privatisation of land, mystification of co-operative structures, etc.

While research and experimentation with pilot projects have very important roles, one cannot escape from an examination of why policies and resolutions are not implemented. Resolutions have been passed on what seems like virtually everything. Successful pilot projects are not generalised. That Africa cannot feed itself is well known. One has to question actual government priorities, which are not necessarily geared to improving people's lives.

Not only officials but also local communities tend to give low priority to rural women. It is the responsibility (and necessity) therefore of women to raise these issues. They can oppose inappropriate technologies or detrimental policies. For example, in Botswana, they succeeded in opposing a commercial beer licence which would have thrown 10,000 women small producers out of work, it was reported.

Why is it only international organisations that seem to take up projects and technologies for rural women while governments give them little priority, it was queried. Increasing food imports and falling export prices are certainly visible, yet the core causes do not seem to be tackled, even though one would think that it would be in the government interest. One sees too often a pattern where irrigation and other land improvements are introduced

and women lose access to that improved land that would have enabled
them to increase, say, rice production.   Or companies are brought
in to increase food production, unsuccessfully, while the actual
food producers receive no support.   But, it was argued, there is
no reason to believe that the State would intervene on behalf of
peasants or women; it may first want to extract more surplus from
women.   In this context, appreciation of the role of the ILO in
evaluating the impact of past interventions, and in improving
inter-actions with States, workers' and employers' organisations,
was mentioned.

There is a chance now to do something in Africa with respect
to women and food, because it is becoming a political problem for
the survival of governments, it was argued.   One should not just
say "food first", but "how" and "for whom".

But there was little illusion concerning the deeper issues
involved.   Women's ideological marginalisation tends to accompany
commercialisation.   Maintaining women in subsistence production
permits payment of a lower wage to men.   Dual exploitation should
not be lost sight of.   Much time is spent in looking for quick,
simple solutions which do not exist, and very little evaluation
is done.   Government may say that food self-sufficiency is the
target and introduce new "high yielding varieties" of plants.
Yet women are rejecting some of them, for very concrete reasons -
e.g. they can increase women's work in weeding and harvesting
without the women receiving the benefit; they may be harder to process and the taste less acceptable. One should examine what such
programmes really mean and their impact, not just listen to what
they sound like.   It is not enough to talk about self-sufficiency
in food while buying all the inputs abroad.   There is a tendency
to neglect local research and information and import foreign
"knowledge".   Progress might be slower but more solid if this
bias were corrected.

Chapter 4

MIGRATION
Presentation: Marie-Angelique Savané

Migration of individuals or families follows a variety of patterns - within rural areas, toward urban areas, for shorter or longer periods of time. But the fundamental reason for migration is typically a search for work.

Focusing on migration over substantial distances and for extended periods of time, one sees that in Africa it has occurred on a large scale at different times in history. There was a move of whole peoples from East to West; some were displaced or expelled, others moved for more direct economic reasons, and of course slavery led to great migration. During the colonial period there was organised migration, for example, of people of Southern Africa to the mines in South Africa, as well as migration, particularly to France, from North and West Africa. State-organised large-scale migration was often linked to expropriation of land to facilitate large-scale farming by White settlers, e.g. in Southern Africa, Algeria and Kenya. Seasonal migration was then encouraged, to provide a labour force for settlers.

Contemporary migration is of a different type, without force, although it is still primarily a case of the rich employers looking for for cheap labour and the poor searching for work. The principal types are organised, provoked and spontaneous migration.

Organised migration is generally related to state policy: e.g. between Senegal and Gabon and with Chad to furnish labour, and with France; when a State decides to develop an underpopulated area, e.g. in Upper Volta, and a large number of people are encouraged to move to the new lands to develop them; and where the development of plantations or extractive industries requires the displacement of the existing population, e.g. in Algeria.

Provoked migration is a result of war or natural disaster, e.g. with the droughts in the Sahel and a number of conflicts which have created enormous refugee populations in Africa, especially in the Horn and Southern Africa.

Spontaneous migration is a result of individual decisions. People come to cities to find work - initially men but now also women - especially in prostitution and domestic service. (Sometimes male

miners are provided with liquor and prostitutes.)   They move across
Africa, sometimes as traders in contraband.   Some peasants, often
the men with their families staying behind (and receiving remittances), moved from West and North Africa to Europe (e.g. France,
Belgium, the Federal Republic of Germany), to do work the Europeans
do not want to do.   And there still are nomads, less touched by
agricultural problems but sometimes in conflict with farmers.

The effect of migration on agriculture has been significant.
There are, for example, plantation enclaves from Upper Volta, in
the Ivory Coast and Ghana and women (many of whom are heads of households) in Southern Africa take care of subsistence production and
also plantations.   The migration of men depends on women maintaining production in their absence, and allows the payment of low
non-family wages to men.   In addition, there are implications for
the choice of crop, e.g. toward manioc (cassava), which is less labour-
intensive.   Women's burden of work tends to become seriously
excessive - e.g. 15-16 hours per day in the Upper Volta - with subsistence and cash crops plus "reproductive" labour.   There are
psychological problems as a result, as well as impoverishment and
deterioration of the soil, requiring even larger capital investment
as a result.

Women who remain behind when men migrate, and who therefore
become in fact heads of households, nevertheless do not acquire the
actual status of household head which would afford them access to
crédit and other resources.   This is a highly important factor in
the deterioration of agriculture and food supply.

When husbands are away for years at a time, there is an effect
on women which is hardly discussed but serious.   Women are thrust
into unaccustomed decision-making, the psychological aspects of
which have been neglected.   Parallel to this is a reinforcement of
patriarchal structures when, e.g. remittances are sent to the head
of the lineage, who controls what the wife receives, and tends to
underestimate what she requires for agricultural production.   There
have been reports from animatrices that heads of lineage object to
women gathering together to discuss issues - a power they have
because of husbands' absence.   Men live as they wish in the cities -
with few responsibilities - while the women face greater restrictions
than before.

Underlying reasons for migration are the prevailing national strategies of development and the international economy (e.g. where mines are developed with foreign capital to meet foreign demand). There are alternatives however. The State could utilise local labour for a different development.

Nevertheless, within the present situation, without talking about fundamental changes in society, there are possibilities for improvement. There could be a large component for women within "integrated rural development" (which could include leisure, child care, etc.). One could focus on supporting women better in what they are doing, e.g. through extension services. Ways could be found to remunerate women for work they are doing. Income-generating activities which are viable could be encouraged.

There is, however, a need for national co-ordination to draw projects for women together into the national plans rather than only encouraging small, discrete, fragmented and uncoordinated efforts.

Discussion

There were many national and regional examples of migration presented.

Some migration has been a result of political instability, e.g. Tanzania received immigrants from Rwanda, Uganda, Angola and Rhodesia (now Zimbabwe). Only the men got employment; there have been attempts to develop women's home-maker roles, including crafts, plus education and co-operatives. There have been some illegal movements - e.g. cattle rustling - even with some men killed and women thus becoming heads of households, and some smuggling of goods (with loss to government of foreign exchange). The Masai and other nomads move to find fodder, taking women and children and interrupting education. There have been attempts (e.g. in Tanzania) to bring nomads together and settle them, providing services. Women are supposed to be included in the village councils and some are running co-operative shops - the result of a deliberate Government effort to provide women with income-earning possibilities. Women move to the village of their husband upon marriage, although some move for economic reasons, with educated women moving to the cities.

In Malawi, however, women own land and marriage is matrilocal (the word for man is stranger, because he has no land rights in his wife's village) - illustrating the variety of African traditions.

In some cases, out-migration of men has strengthened women's traditional land rights.　Land belonged to the tribe, not to individuals, but there is a trend toward privatisation and some women have gained the right to sell when male relatives were absent.　Men (e.g. officials and officers) are typically the buyers of land.　With the sharp reduction in male migration (reportedly 300,000 to 24,000 in one year), men's interest in the land may intensify.

In Lesotho, Botswana and Swaziland, where there has been a great deal of male out-migration, it is possible to hire tractors to replace male labour.　The effect has been to increase women's work as more land is cleared and they are also responsible for the other tasks. But women do not control the labour process - they have to wait for men to apply for credit, hire tractors, etc.　In addition, male migration has meant that women are more involved in animal husbandry (although they do not own the cattle), in spite of taboos with respect to cattle and fertility.

The World Bank has done detailed sectoral studies in a number of countries, recently Lesotho.　There, with male migration, women were left with three-quarters of the work but without control of land or of decisions concerning spending of remittances or even hiring of tractors.　And, because marriage is patrilocal, women are isolated in their husbands' villages.　To provide advice to the Government, the Bank looked at the likely impact of cutting off male migration.

Less is said about separate female migration.　In Lesotho, for example, young girls are recruited in villages and taken to towns to work in factories under inadequate conditions (sub-minimum wages). After working for three to five years, they become unemployed, often with nowhere to go except into prostitution.

Agriculture in Zambia has suffered from several kinds of migration.　Male migrants came to work in mines to the neglect of native agriculture while settlers displaced local farmers in areas near the road built to serve the mines.　Now, many men have migrated to the cities to find employment as there has been little attention to rural transport and industry, health care and other services. If there were a number of growth points in rural areas (as Zimbabwe is planning), with local production, processing and consumption linked, there would probably be a reduction in male migration to cities and in separate female migration for prostitution.

Another kind of migration occurs with the shift of people to new settlements (as in Ethiopia), often without adequate water or employment opportunities. There can be tremendous hardship when people are uprooted and lose traditional networks, and no alternative structures are provided. Ideally, the provision of facilities should coincide with the migration.

In Sierra Leone, many men, hoping to get rich quickly, abandon farms in search of diamonds. Very few got rich; most go on for years or die in the search. Women are left behind to cope with their families on their own, while men tend to father children in different areas as they move.

It is clear that both migration and return have important implications for women, the sexual division of labour and agricultural production. With privatisation and growing markets for land, women's traditional rights may be threatened. An end to migration can also be very disruptive. There are examples of the return of disabled males and of growing alcoholism. Pensions are essentially non-existent. South Africa is moving to phase out migration and its southern African neighbours have been trying to discourage migration and the associated dependence. There needs to be more attention to alternatives for women as well as men in rural areas, to reduce the need for migration (into prostitution, etc.), and greater efforts in support of women refugees. Yet government programmes targeted to women are mostly aimed at their nurturing roles and do not benefit them in their principal economic activities. For example, instead of programmes for alcoholism among women (suffering as a result of an end to male migration), there was a programme for "better living" in which women were told to be calm, accept men's problems, and create harmony.

Such programmes are a bad example of the handling of social changes that accompany an end to migration. There needs to be a careful assessment of prospective transformation in rural areas and a focus on the impact on women to ensure that they and their productive work are not unduly harmed in the process.

Chapter 5

INCOME-GENERATING ACTIVITIES[*]
Presentation: Jasleen Dhamija

There is going to be a substantial increase in the female labour force between now and the year 2000, which will not readily be absorbed without a substantial effort at many levels, including training (see Chapter 2, Part II).   Yet it must be recognised that income for the sake of income is not enough.   Do projects perpetuate exploitation or lead to self-fulfilment, self-sufficiency and viable economic activities?

Perhaps a third of households are headed by women, who thus face particular disadvantages in generating income.   They have exceptional responsibilities but not authority, particularly in the sense of legal status.   A woman may not even be able to stand in court unless accompanied by a male, however young.   She may not be allowed to borrow without permission.   And so on.

Development workers seldom reach and really communicate with rural people, and if they do, it is to carry out projects designed elsewhere.   In addition, such workers including extension agents are often overburdened and poorly prepared for their task.   With respect to women, they tend to suggest actions - such as providing milk or eggs for children, using soap, etc. - for which the women lack money, while ignoring women's productive roles and failing to support them.   Hardly ever is an integrated view taken of a woman and her needs.

Women in the subsistence sector are particularly neglected by extension programmes.   One can see how acute their needs are when, for example, a woman walks 10 kilometres to sell a few eggs and a squash, so that she can buy basic necessities such as salt and oil.

There is a need to support both formal and informal activities, those based on traditional sectors and also non-traditional, in services as well as production.   It is not enough to wait until men move out of an activity into something more remunerative, for women to acquire a new skill or trade.

---

[*] The Seminar agenda included an item on "organisation" rather than "income-generating activities".   However, the subject of organisation underlay much of the discussion on all topics, including policy.   And there was a lively interest in the subject of income-generating activities, which was also pursued during the sessions in the course of the field trip, and is thus given the prominence in this Report that it held in the Seminar.

It is essential for women's participation in institutions and training to be increased, recognising the constraints they face. It has been estimated that 85 per cent of the beneficiaries even of non-formal agricultural training are male (90 per cent in the case of institutional programmes). Only 2.4 per cent of those in vocational institutions are women. Even in services where women have been traditionally important, such as marketing in West Africa, women may predominate in petty trade but they are pushed out, marginalised, in trading firms and modern marketing.

Lip service is often paid to a balanced economy, but most governments still plan for capital-intensive industrialisation, which also encourages urbanisation and male migration.

There is a need to break out of the concepts of masculine/ feminine tasks, and consider why, e.g. sewing by hand is for women and by machine is for men; why pottery making by hand is for women and with a wheel is for men. It is true that one should recognise taboos, but one should also try to break taboos.

The ILO/ECA regional project on handicrafts and small industries for women, with the African Training and Research Center for Women, has attempted to play a catalytic role in a number of countries.

In Egypt, women in several villages were assisted in developing traditional skills and marketing the products. But service, credit and training aspects were neglected. In Tunisia, the same idea was picked up but in a more organised way - preceded by a careful survey of materials, and training was linked with institutions providing services - so this one was more successful. In Lesotho, 30 people were trained in the weaving of high quality rugs and tapestry and pottery making over five years, but difficulties arose because the co-operative was not organised. Tie and dye activities have been started in a number of countries. In Ethiopia and the Somali Republic, women were trained in groups and given business training, which was more successful. Some traditional barriers have been broken down, including within non-traditional areas. One has to create awareness among policy makers and links with institutions (including those supplying credit) and women's organisations, but there also is need for a data base.

Discussion

Most policy makers are scared of data, it was stated. Most planning is based on assumptions and very old - even colonial - data. AAWORD was identifying critical areas for data collection to improve the planning process. One of the aims of research is to sensitise decision makers, to make them understand that rural development programmes are not helping women, that "women's programmes" are not necessarily good (particularly when they have a home economics orientation), and that policies and plans should and can be modified.

The query was raised whether integrated programmes or specific programmes and projects targeted for women are more appropriate. Since the presentations have generally concluded that not much, if any, progress has been made toward equality between men and women, with women being excluded from much of income-earning work, what are the implications? Perhaps it is more appropriate to focus on some specific aspects of particular importance - e.g. women's access to land, doing something directly about providing land titles, and introducing something specific about access to appropriate education - rather than promoting integrated, broader policies.

Many projects are irrelevant, it was argued, because foreign experts come to a country, consult only a few officials and write up a project. When such people come, they should be required to have a sociologist accompany them and consult the people. For women, the target must be greater purchasing power as the only way to be really free, it was argued.

In Senegal, the Secretariat d'Etat à la Promotion Humaine has been involved since 1963 with the promotion of women. Initially, the focus was on social issues, housekeeping and nutrition. There was a disequilibrium created as women's productive activities were not being adequately supported; there were few animatrices compared to animateurs and they lacked technical support. In 1975, they evaluated what women were doing. Education in nutrition and house-keeping was not meeting real needs (they knew how to cook). Many women were working in the fields but were given the idea of starting sewing rather than being assisted as agriculturalists. Some women had meetings and decided to reject the sewing programmes. It was found that programmes should be reoriented. Producers' groups were recommended at first, and then the idea progressed in some zones to women's groups (groupement de la promotion feminine) which take a more integrated view of women.

A number of projects were started with the help of various international organisations and bilateral donors to assist women within agriculture, including cassava, vegetable gardening, preserving and grinding, as well as animal husbandry, in each case incorporating training. There have still been inadequate results with respect to infrastructure and credit but progress has been made at the level of national planning, it was stated, as particular attention to women was inscribed in the Fifth Development Plan. But detailed information on women's real needs was still lacking - animal raising was promoted among women with no tradition or interest in it, intensive vegetable production was promoted where women did not have access to sufficient water, mills were introduced which they could not repair, etc.

One of the basic problems with "income-generating activities", it was argued, was that they do not generate much income. In spite of goodwill, they seem to be adding to women's work burden. They may be well-intentioned but as they are not based on proper economic analysis, costing, marketing surveys, etc., they are not well founded. In reply, it was argued that some are superficial but some do work, although they may take several years. Yet even where a government promises to continue support after international project support comes to an end, they fail to pick up the projects.

There seemed to be a need to involve counterpart funding and technical assistance at an early stage to avoid some of these problems. It is fair to criticise the dependence on outside fund-ing and the problems that arise when funding comes to an end. But, on the other hand, it has been stated that only the international agencies seem to be really interested in projects for women, and that such interest was invaluable in pursuing women's development. There was a kind of vicious circle, even where no expatriates were brought in. Government tends to expect external funding for women's projects and do not carefully plan women's projects themselves.

If one looks at the duration of women's projects, whether funded internally or externally, it is typically one or two years and one cannot expect to change a villager's life in such a short period. It may be doing women a service to say openly that such projects do not work. There are many development projects which have been going on for ten, even 30 years, without many results. Extension work for men, after about 20 years, seems to have borne little fruit. Projects should

have a life of at least ten years, it was argued, with monitoring
and follow-up built in to see that goals and methods are adjusted
as it progresses.

With some projects, it is evident that they are going to fail
before they start.   One should not be attracted to projects just
because money is available.   One needs to know and consult the
community first.   More educated people should become involved, to
assist in developing momentum for more appropriate projects and
encouraging local commitment to relevant programmes.

The importance of involving men as well as women was suggested.
An integrated view then takes account of women's domestic as well as
economic roles, since women's projects will tend to result in lower
productivity and efficiency than men's so long as women have dual
roles and men only one.   Governments should take a more active role
in seeking solutions to the burden of domestic roles, it was argued.

There also has to be care in delineating the target group since
there are different strata among women.   There may not always be
really rich people in rural areas but there is differentiation.
Some women, for example, may hire male labour from a lower class.
One should seek to assist disadvantaged groups with common
interests.

Chapter 6

POLICY IMPLICATIONS
Presentation: Danielle Bazin

It is not evident that reality reflects "development as if women mattered".   Men and women are affected by development and both should be agents of development, but we know that this is not in fact happening.   So it is necessary to focus on women and where they are - especially in rural areas.   One needs, now, to move towards "development through women", supporting women to become agents of change.

In order to realise this, actions are required in both agriculture and small industries sectors.   For more appropriate agricultural development, women must have access to land.   There have been many instances where women have been displaced from land once it has been improved, although in a village in the Niger, the women revolted and demanded parcels of newly irrigated land be given to them, not just to the "family" - and they obtained individual rights to the land.   From a policy perspective, irrigation schemes must pay attention to women's rights and needs if they are to result in beneficial agricultural development.

Women also need to receive training, including as extension agents, in order to extend and popularise agricultural knowledge at the local level, through working with village women.   Agricultural credit is essential for raising production, but women generally lack the guarantees requested by banks - in particular, land.   Some progress has been seen where groups of women are formed around credit or revolving funds, modern versions of an old custom in various areas.

Mechanisation could aid women in their work, but the general trend is for innovations to ignore women and support only men. There is some training of men and women for local-level extension supported by the UN, showing, e.g. how women can also operate and repair machines, with demonstrations that can be repeated when the trainees go to the villages.   So women can show other women how to manage the machines, to go against the trend to exclude them.

In the small industries sector, there is considerable scope for promoting the processing of foodstuffs and other agricultural products (e.g. staples and items such as gari, attiéké and palm oil). There are possibilities for semi-industrial development based on

community resources.   In some cases, there is a basis for promoting
artisanal work in rural areas.

And, of course, women are important beneficiaries of improvements in water supply, housing and technologies to lessen the burden
of unpaid work.

There have been many recommendations to governments and
international organisations but a strategy to put them into practice
is lacking.   Group pressure is needed to influence actual policies.
There are groups at international, regional, national and other
levels which can be encouraged to use their influence more effectively.   There is considerable potential through solidarity and
networking among committed women and men.

Discussion

There was agreement with the importance of focusing on
strategies - otherwise resolutions are only for self-satisfaction.
But a query was raised with respect to structures.   Networking and
groups are important, but where they do not exist, there may be women's
bureaux.   Are such special units perhaps even counter-productive,
offering discrete, unlinked women's programmes to the detriment of
the required policy changes needed, which have just been presented?
Perhaps it would be preferable to have women's units within all
ministries, to pursue positive action on behalf of women in, e.g.
ministries of commerce, agriculture, forestry, etc.

Sometimes governments seem to think that they have discharged
their responsibility by setting up women's bureaux.   When one
bureau or organisation is accepted as the national organisation for
women, the result may be to leave out other even larger organisations
which should get involved.   There is also a tendency, it was argued,
for assistance to women to be channelled through that accepted
national organisation while excluding others wich are doing
effective work at the grass-roots level.   Failure to link up with
the latter constitutes a great loss, because they remain less
effective than they could be if they were to receive adequate
support and encouragement.   These structural questions need to be
examined frankly.

Botswana provides an interesting illustration.   There is, it
was reported, a commission on women in which are included all
ministries or their representatives.   This commission was able to

block the licensing of a factory that would have thrown 10,000 women out of work, so it had some demonstrated influence.

Where States have taken the step of setting up ministries or bureaux for women, they should be made to work and should be given financial resources (may be reorganising their conceptions) before other structures are set up, it was argued.

Another participant felt, however, that a stock-taking of what has been done by women's bureaux would probably reveal a negative result. Bureaux dealing only with women do not seem to be working effectively, nor taking up the particular issues concerning poor and peasant women. The mechanism needs to be rethought, with a study on the question of women in the context of all ministries. It may well be better to have special units within all ministries. However, effectiveness may also depend on their level within the ministry. Or maybe both are needed. Units could pursue programmes within each ministry, but a special bureau or ministry may be necessary to promote women's programmes and interests.

An example of a relatively effective women's bureau was given from a Caribbean country, under a prime minister's office and represented on the planning commission. Having some political influence and presence on the Commission which processes foreign assistance, it is able to raise women's issues directly at a key point in the processing of projects.

Tanzania also has a unit in the Prime Minister's office, with workers at all levels. Some rural development assistants are trained, but they tend not to stay in rural areas, so the presence at the grass-roots level is limited. There is also a national women's organisation, which represents women at local, district and national levels. It sets up economic activities for its members, but most women are not members. Sometimes the organisation is used for individual advantage, it was stated.

The phenomenon of organisations used to the advantage of ambitious individuals is true for men as well as women, however. It is a sociological phenomenon in most groups for some to take the lead and others to follow. It should be recognised that many existing structures serve to exploit part of the population, it was argued. One should be realistic, and at the same time try to reorient and use the structures for meeting the people's needs.

There was some further discussion on the issues of groups, organisations and networking. There are, it was recognised, many women's groups which do not have links with many important aspects of women's interests. Nevertheless, solidarity of women's groups should be encouraged. Informal groups need a means of co-ordinating and linking. International organisations may be able to help in this regard. They also have a key role in raising issues, it was argued, since much project designing does go on at that level. Pressure groups with a political base or within political parties may be another means that should be promoted. These are approaches to breaking prejudices and reducing information gaps as well.

Perhaps more could be done at the level of trade unions, according to several participants. One should consider women's role in them. In Africa, it is very rare to find women in trade unions and working for women's interests.

Experience with co-operatives also seemed to be much less than satisfactory from women's viewpoint. Even where women are organised in co-operatives, they lack managerial and management skills. Credit is an important aspect of whatever organisations are formed.

Given the maleness of administrations and the extent of actual discrimination against women, it is necessary to involve men, it was stated. Some men·can be conscientised and instrumentalised to raise the prominence of women's issues on a par with men's interests. Another participant, however, argued that the emphasis should be on special women's groups and organisations because women are relegated to poorer jobs and lower levels within integrated ones. The marginalisation of women is in fact a problem of society as a whole, with an impact on women, and cannot be "solved" in isolation. Putting women in a ghetto can therefore prevent a solution to their problems, while raising the visibility of their problems at higher levels can contribute to solutions. One must recognise how fundamental a change that would be since women are presently subjected to a mode of production controlled by men, it was stated.

In order to assist in developing strategies, the conscientisation of officials is relevant. Some specific actions taken by the World Bank were reported. For example, in one country it has been assisting the government to set up an administrative unit in the ministry concerned with women, for the purpose of reviewing the projects of other ministries. One of the first to come up was forestry, involving fuel and improved stores, and it was brought to the attention of the women's ministry. In another country, it was seen that an irrigation project would cause women not only to lose their land rights but also to take on additional work in weeding. A condition was attached to the loan requiring a particular share of the proceeds from the irrigated land to go to women. If one brings together agronomists, technology specialists and local representatives, it may be possible to develop downstream processing of agricultural waste, e.g. to increase employment in rural areas.

Training, however, is wasted if it is not linked to planned use of the skills to be acquired. An example was given of women who were trained in using tractors, but were so ridiculed when they returned to their villages that they stopped using them. An effort in providing some orientation to the villagers about the new role of these women might have made a difference.

There also needs to be more of an effort among social scientists. Articles concerned with women's issues are not published in the leading journals. The impact of existing knowledge is therefore **constrained**. The roster on African social scientists being prepared may lead to some greater awareness of the potential contribution. Women, particularly those who are social scientists, must review their own organisations and strategies. They also will be guilty if the present structures continue into the 1990s.

Some may complain that there is a lack of connection between research and planners and that, **for example**, planners do not read the results of research. But, it was argued, much of research provides information and analysis but does not indicate policy implications. Researchers must themselves help to establish the linkages, with the help of international organisations. This Seminar was seen as a contribution to this process.

Chapter 7

CONCLUSIONS OF THE ILO TRIPARTITE AFRICAN REGIONAL SEMINAR, RURAL DEVELOPMENT AND WOMEN, DAKAR, SENEGAL, 15-19 JUNE 1981

Rural women in Africa make up a disproportionate part of the labour force in subsistence agriculture, and they participate in cash crop production and are hired as seasonal labourers on plantations. In addition, women are almost solely responsible for food processing, conservation and storage, housework, maintenance and child care. Existing census data greatly underestimate women's labour input into agricultural production, as a result of being based on a faulty conceptualisation of "work", intra-household relations and the labour process subsumed under housework.

Consequently, national plans and agricultural policies perceive women only as housewives and mothers and not as farmers. As a result, most women are denied access to land, credit, extension services, technology and other forms of institutional support, and therefore women's time-consuming and laborious tasks are characterised by low productivity and wastage. Low productivity impedes attainment of the goal of self-sufficiency in food production, and the burden of the multiple tasks women are forced to undertake has an impact on their well-being, that of their children and the family as a whole.

In view of the concern of governments to increase food production and the income and well-being of the population, rural development strategies have to reconsider the role of women in rural production and distribution so that planners can devise strategies that would simultaneously ameliorate the working and living conditions of rural women and raise their productivity. The successful implementation of these new strategies, however, will depend on the recognition, strengthening and/or restructuring of grass root organisations which will have to be involved in the planning and execution of projects.

Research and data collection

Government agencies (particularly planning units) and research institutes, women's organisations and international agencies, should include women's interests in national research programmes as well as undertake participatory research focusing on the changing role and status of women. Research on, inter alia, agricultural production, the introduction of new technology and settlement and irrigation schemes, as well as pre-feasibility studies and project evaluations have to pay particular attention to the changing division of labour by sex, intra-household relations and obligations in addition to changes in ownership, production, income distribution and consumption. While examining the impact of these changes on rural men and women, attention has to be paid to the impact of these processes on the different strata of the rural population.

In line with reconsideration of rural development strategies, there is a great need to re-examine concepts and assumptions that presently underlie data collection and analysis. In this regard, concepts such as "household", "housework", "work", "employment" and "farmer" will have to be reconceptualised so as to reflect the actual nature of the labour processes and social relations currently prevailing in rural Africa. In addition to indicating men's and women's contribution to the rural economy and the survival of the household, such a framework would permit a better understanding of new phenomena such as female-headed households and female seasonal workers. Finally, both sectoral and national-level data should always be disaggregated by sex as well as by age and economic status.

Such a breakdown would demonstrate the contribution of both men and women to production as well as strengthen efforts towards the elimination of inequalities based on sex and focus the attention of policy makers and planners on incorporating these issues in policy and programme design. Action-oriented research would also contribute to these ends.

Women in food production

Presently, Africa is faced with a serious food crisis and most national plans have given priority to the need to increase food production. Typically, rural women are the principal cultivators of food crops, and they process, preserve and store food. Therefore, any effort to increase food production would have to first of all recognise women as the cultivators and target groups of rural development programmes. Yet frequently these programmes unwittingly place an additional work burden on women without assisting them to produce and process food. To this end, priority should be given to legal measures that would give women equitable access to land. Furthermore, women should have access to credit, extension services,

improved tools and all other inputs that increase productivity.
They should also have full access to co-operatives and other rural
workers' organisations.   More women extension agents should be
recruited and trained to teach agricultural techniques.   The goal
of increasing food production also necessitates the introduction of
time and labour-saving technology in other areas of women's work
such as processing, preservation, storage and cooking.   Likewise,
infrastructure services such as clean, accessible water and fuel
supply, child care centres and health clinics will have direct
implications on the acquisition of new and better skills by rural
women, on their health situation and the overall well-being of
their children.   Time saved from these various tasks can also create
the condition for remunerative employment activities which would
increase the household's income.   However, measures should be taken
to ensure that surplus accruing from this increased productivity is
not extracted by men.

Rural modernisation

In view of the growing trend towards social differentiation,
modernisation projects should not be premised on a homogeneous rural
population, nor households as units of convergent interests where all
benefits and responsibilities are shared equally.   Modernisation
accentuates social differentiation and transforms intra-household
relations.

Therefore, land reform schemes which require registration,
individualisation of land and other forms of changes in ownership of
land should involve registration of land in the name of husbands and
wives (and just women in the case of women-headed households).
Similarly, rights to the ownership of land should be granted to each
individual, regardless of gender, and joint titles should be given to
husbands and wives.   Along with ownership and legal titles to land,
modernisation schemes should ensure women's rights to the use and
management of land and all other complementary inputs as well as
equal access to returns from agricultural surplus.

Furthermore, prior to the introduction of settlement projects,
irrigation schemes and integrated rural development programmes, pre-
feasibility studies should be conducted to determine the impact of
such projects on households of different socio-economic strata, the
sexual division of labour and the distribution of resources within
the household.   Similarly, the impact of the introduction of

pre- and post-harvest technology on different households and on men and women and the links between their different tasks in the production cycle, should also be closely studied.

In view of the limited and concentrated nature of the benefits to a limited number of households, alternative remunerative employment possibilities should be created for men and women of the rural poor whose livelihood is negatively affected by such changes. Present cash incomes are inadequate and projections indicate that agriculture will be unable to absorb the growing female labour force. This makes it imperative to develop non-farm activities enabling women to gain remunerative employment and new or upgraded skills. For an effective impact, it is essential to develop educational programmes that would lead to vocational and technical training directed towards women in traditional and non-traditional areas of activities. Women should have access to institutions concerned with food processing, small-scale industrial development, credit and other sectors existing and being developed in the countries. Employment opportunities have to be accompanied by commensurate wages and good working conditions. Governments, trade unions and employers should implement existing conventions concerning wages and working conditions as well as formulate laws that would ensure the access of rural women to employment, equal pay and safe working conditions that take their maternal role into account. Laws should also guarantee their rights to unionise so as to ensure that women workers obtain their rights and raise their consciousness. Trade unions have a particular responsibility to educate women workers concerning their rights and to assist them in obtaining training.

Migration

Men and women migrate individually and also collectively as family units. The underdevelopment of the regions from which men migrate (leaving women as de facto heads of families) and the decline in food production necessitate the introduction of projects that would address themselves to women's needs and provide them with agricultural extension, education and other services. In regions where rural resettlements have been introduced, it is important to identify women's actual labour input into agricultural production and to recognise women as farmers in their own right and not just as assistants. This recognition has to be accompanied with efforts to alleviate women's domestic responsibilities.

In southern Africa, the gradual reduction of male migration and the return of migrants from the mines of South Africa back to their countries have brought about changes in household relations and the organisation of production as regards the sexual division of labour, access to land and credit.   The legacy of long-term migration manifests itself at the level of familial relations in problems such as alcoholism and other psychological and physical handicaps from which long-term male migrants suffer, and these necessitate a series of accommodations on the part of rural women. Given these conditions, there is a need for an integrated approach to rural development that would take all the socio-economic, psychological and cultural dimensions of these problems into account.

The growing complementary trend of female migration from the countryside to the towns results, given the rate of unemployment and underemployment in urban areas, in migrant women becoming housemaids and prostitutes.   To counter such trends, women's projects and employment opportunities have to be created in rural areas.

Women's organisations

Women have formed organisations in response to the difficult conditions of existence in the rural areas.   There are various forms of organisations which are based on traditional informal associations, organisations formed by the State or international agencies, inter alia.   In the last few years, national machineries, commissions or ministries to coordinate women's issues have been created to identify, evaluate and ameliorate the condition of women.

In a number of countries, there are no laws that recognise the right of women to organise.   Passing and implementation of such laws and ensuring that women are informed would permit rural women to organise in order to participate in the planning and execution of rural development projects and programmes.   Women's points of view will not be recognised if they are not organised and represented in decision-making bodies.

Women will also have to be integrated in trade unions of agricultural workers and peasant associations within which they can form pressure groups for meeting their specific needs, e.g. in the formulation of labour laws regarding equal wages and basic needs, etc.   Workers' education is an important component of this process.

In places where no laws exist and where they are not executed, laws should be passed and implemented allowing women to be members of co-operatives and other rural workers' organisations, and to benefit from their advantages such as agricultural credit, seeds, fertilisers and other technological inputs and extension services.

PART II

BACKGROUND PAPERS

OVERVIEW OF THE PAPERS

The papers prepared for this Seminar cover a wide range of
activities and trends, and each has its own orientation toward the
problems facing a particular society regarding the participation of
women in rural development.   Yet they echo a common theme.   All the
women described in the studies are in some way caught in a squeeze
between their responsibilities to themselves and their families
(which are often increasing), the resources available to them (which
do not show a corresponding increase but often a decrease) and their
limited freedom to undertake new activities in order to survive
under the new conditions.

Women all over Africa are responsible for the provisioning of
certain basic household needs and the performance of a number of
tasks necessary to their families' survival, including many highly
labour-intensive forms of food processing (described by Stevens,
Date-Bah and Traoré in considerable detail), child care, cooking,
some handicrafts, such as soap-making in Sierra Leone (Stevens),
and often subsistence agriculture.

At the same time, many of these same women must meet the
increasing cash requirements that accompany the provisioning of their
families' needs, both for goods they can no longer supply for
themselves, such as types of food and fuel, and for new needs, such
as education and modern health services.   Both Nene and Traoré
describe situations in which women are increasingly strained to
meet new cash needs, yet they are finding the environment hostile to
their attempts to do so.

Among the factors that contribute to these growing responsibilities is the trend toward male out-migration, which leaves women
entirely responsible for their families' subsistence needs, including
their agricultural activities, income-generating activities, household maintenance, child care and food processing.   Many South African
women have already found themselves in such a situation, and have
been forced to make some dramatic changes in their lives in order
to cope with their new responsibilities, as Nene describes in the
case of the South African petty traders.

A less dramatic form of reduction in men's contribution to
their families' survival is the movement of men out of the subsistence

sector and into cash cropping, public works projects and agricultural
wage labour.   The men may continue to live at home and contribute
minimal amounts to family maintenance, but women become entirely
responsible for subsistence agriculture and other activities that
had been shared previously.   Traoré's study of the effects of the
development of palm oil plantations, utilising male labour, decreasing
male input in manioc (cassava) production and other household and
agricultural chores, clearly convinces us of the overly large
burden women must labour under when they become responsible for
both-their own and their men's traditional tasks.

In some of the studies, it is also apparent that increasing
poverty is pressuring the traditional extended family networks that
normally provide a form of informal social security to individuals
lacking adequate means to support themselves.   Under new and
formidable demands, these systems are breaking down, leaving the
women without any barrier to utter deprivation.   Again Nene describes
a clear example of this situation in South Africa, but some of the
other studies also indicate similar occurrences.   It is worth noting
here that this phenomenon was also raised in the Tripartite Asian
Regional Seminar on Rural Development and Women.

The development programmes these studies examine do not, by and
large, improve the rural women's positions vis à vis access to
resources and economic needs.   Rather, they have in several places
had the effect of further restricting the alternatives available to
women and draining a number of important resources from them, and
sometimes from the rural areas altogether.   Most significantly,
women have repeatedly lost access to income-generating activities,
which are taken over by men or machines, and frequently a combination of both.   Dhamija, Traoré, Nene, Stevens and Date-Bah all
describe the phenomenon of men taking over a previously female
activity, usually with the aid of machines and improved technology
introduced by their governments or an outside aid agency.   Typical
of these occurrences is the example Dhamija gives of women entrepreneurs beginning a fish smoking operation in Senegal.   When the
Government moved in with aid in the form of improved technology and
ovens for fish smoking, the operation was handed over to men, and
the women were displaced.   Allaghi's study of a resettlement
village in the Libyan Arab Jamahariya tells of a somewhat different
problem, that of women losing access to income-generating activities
due to lack of access to the raw materials in their new setting.

Land, as an essential resource in most rural areas, is also increasingly scarce for women relative to men.   Agricultural and land reforms have at times concentrated rights to ownership in the hands of men.   These studies include examples from the Ivory Coast (Traoré), where much of the land formerly used for subsistence agriculture by the women was seized for use in a palm oil plantation, and Senegal (Ba et al), where the entire country underwent redistricting and land reform, and men received legal title to a great deal of land which they had previously controlled under traditional land tenure systems which had required them to allow women access to their land.   Through the granting of legal land title to men, women no longer had the right to demand access to their relatives' land.   In addition, the number of landless families increased as a result of the registration of land in the name of those in a position to manipulate the legal measures.

Associated with the lack of land access, women are finding that they have limited and decreasing access to such resources as fuel-wood and other goods that had been freely available.   This is partly due to their loss of land privileges, but also to the privatisation of communal and public land areas, deforestation and the spread of urban and industrial areas.   In response, women must either buy the goods or travel greater and greater distances in order to find them.   In many cases, they must simply do without.

These studies also highlight several cases where development programmes that demand the participation of men and children (usually in primary education), have caused women to lose the ability to command their labour.   According to the findings of Nene, Traoré and Longhurst, women who had previously been able to rely on their male family members and children to perform a task or provide them with a commodity are no longer able to do so.

Another frequent shortcoming of the development programmes described here is their failure to provide viable alternative employ-ment or income-generating activities for rural women.   Many of the activities included in rural development programmes focus on a misperception of women's traditional roles and activities, aimed at home economics and handicrafts.

Where women's activities are included in rural development programmes with the goal of increasing their cash income, the activities that are promoted are usually an extension of the women's

household work, handicrafts and food processing for the market, and
are often labour-intensive, low technology operations.   In addition,
these activities are rarely integrated into the larger rural
economy, and essential transportation and marketing infrastructure
may be lacking.   Often a market for the goods the women produce
does not even exist within a reasonable distance, yet distant
planners do not take that into account in selecting women's
activities.   Allaghi gives the example of a women's programme that
promotes knitting, producing a commodity mal-suited to the hot
environment in which the women live.   Thus, women's ability to
exploit their productivity in the cash economy is severely limited.
Dhamija presents a very convincing argument on the costs of such a
type of "integration" of women into rural development.   It is
necessary, she says, "to break out of the meaningless distinctions
which have been created between skills associated with men and
women".

Within the activities that women traditionally perform and the
rural development activities they are expected to participate in,
improved technologies and infrastructure have failed to ease the
burden of their work.   A common problem is the lack of extension
services and training programmes for women.   In most areas, extension
programmes do not reach women, but concentrate on men instead.   The
fact that there are few institutions that actually carry out research
and development on improved technologies and methods for women's
work is partially responsible for the fact that these programmes
do not target women.   When we consider the increasingly heavy
demands on their time and energies due to the growing responsibilities
they carry, the need for such improvements are clear, and it is not
surprising that rural African women often labour up to 16 hours
a day and cannot afford the luxury of leisure time or activities.

Another problem women encounter is the lack of credit available
to them.   Even where improved technologies exist and women have
access to them, they often cannot afford to take part or to utilise
the inputs they require due to an inability to obtain credit.
Again, most credit that is available in rural Africa is channelled
toward men.   In addition, infrastructure of various sorts exists in
only limited areas, and women frequently suffer special problems that
could be solved with a wider introduction of health, education,
sanitation and transportation infrastructure.   One example given by
Akande deals with water provision in rural areas.   Not only would

piped water save the entire community from illness that results from
unsanitary water supplies and the lost productivity that ensues, but
women would be saved the collection time and the time and energy
devoted to the care of the sick people.   Yet irrigating male-owned
land for commercial crop production is likely to get higher priority.

Most authors attribute the failure of development programmes to
reach and include women to the failure to identify the correct target
group and the needs of that group on a policy level.   This failure,
they find, is a result of several factors, many of which have had
the further effect of restricting women in their attempts to meet
their own and their families' needs in changing societies, independently
of their effects on development policies.

A most common problem is that of blindness on the part of male,
urban and foreign planners toward the important role and activities
of rural African women.   Virtually all the studies in some way
encounter this phenomenon - a lack of understanding on the govern
ment and aid agency level, of women's responsibilities, abilities,
needs and the restrictions, in terms of family commitment and the
unbalanced distribution of resources under which they must operate.
The studies carried out in South Africa (Nene), the Libyan Arab
Jamahiriya (Allaghi), Sierra Leone (Stevens) and Ghana (Date-Bah)
all highlight this lack of understanding with examples of the
dichotomy between the women's needs and the kind of "participation"
expected of them under the existing programmes.   According to Nene,
most of the petty traders included in her study participate in the
activity because they perceive it as the only alternative to starvation for them and their families.   Yet the State and the social
environment are openly hostile to their activities and their attempts
to survive thereby - which indicates something more than blindness.

In many of the studies, the causes of "blindness" are
clearly evident, although they are not directly approached.   Most
authors see misunderstanding emerging from ignorance and indifference
toward a sector of the population of which they have little or no
experience, knowledge or understanding.   Mernissi and Tadesse,
however, both go beyond implicit treatment of the causes and deal
explictly with what they see as some of the major reasons for and
problems with the orientation of many policy-makers.

Everywhere in Africa, women are constricted by the remnants of
the traditional perceptions of women's role and the sexual division
of labour.   These constraints are often built into development
projects, but they also harm women who are trying to survive

under the changes introduced into their communities and areas
through the process of industrialisation and integration into the
world economy.   Ideologies, which may never have assigned women
a place commensurate with the responsibilities associated with
their social and economic roles, but which under traditional
conditions did not restrict them from carrying out those roles and
meeting those responsibilities, have become severely crippling to
women in their attempts to meet those responsibilities under new
conditions and have endangered the entire rural community.   Several
powerful examples are available from the works included here.

In Sierra Leone, according to Stevens, the traditional division
of labour is built around the ideology of dependence and inter-
dependence.   In some areas, women are not supposed to live alone
or be able to support themselves and their children independently -
that is, without the aid of men.   Yet new conditions have forced
many women to take economic responsibility for their families, and
they are finding it very difficult to do so given the traditional
division of labour and the communities' ideas concerning the proper
role and activities of women.

In Morocco, Mernissi finds that the belief that women ought not
be economic actors continually hinders their participation in the
emerging economic institutions and processes and forces them into
positions of dependence on men, leaving them open to exploitation.

In addition to the failure of development programmes and the
limiting effects of divisions of labour, stratification (which
often accompanies development and the integration of the domestic
economy into the world economy) has led to several social changes
which have adversely affected the position of women in many rural
areas.   The immediate effect of stratification is to increase the
distance between the rural poor and the urban elites, who are, by
and large, the policy-makers and planners.   The radically different
lifestyles between these groups leads planners to build into rural
development programmes women's roles that are based on the role of
the wealthy urban housewife and completely unsuited to the
responsibilities and resources of poor rural women.   Again, we
refer to the case of the Libyan women in the resettlement village
examined in the Allaghi study who were taught knitting, an activity
considered feminine and appropriate by the planners living some
distance away, but which was almost totally useless to the women
living in the hot Sahara.

Mernissi and Longhurst are both concerned with the spread of
beliefs in the restriction and seclusion of women, which they
associate with the effects of stratification and the increasing
standard of living of one part of the population relative to the
others.   In order to demonstrate wealth, it is becoming
more and more prestigious to seclude women among the Moslem Hausa
of Nigeria, according to Longhurst.   Mernissi looks at a number of
trends affecting different classes' perceptions of women's
role at different historical moments.   A trend she finds
in Morocco, which is increasingly important in the determina-
tion of ideas concerning women, is the spread of Western
influence both through the urban elite and through the growing
capacity of mass media to reach the rural poor directly.

Tadesse also looks at the effects of stratification and
particularly the differences between rural and urban areas and
lifestyles.   She brings up the issue of the squeeze on the rural
sector as a whole, particularly the agricultural sector.   This
sector often produces primary products for export, upon which the
urban sector depends for the generation of foreign exchange in
order to support the imports of both luxury goods and foreign
technology and industrial inputs.   Within this squeeze, she
remarks that women as unpaid and underpaid labourers are strongly
affected.   They perform activities necessary to both the production
of the export products and the survival of the rural populations,
but the urban planners, who benefit from the low-cost production
of the export goods have strong incentive not to recognise their
role or to remunerate their activities.   Resources are consistently
channelled out of these sectors and into industry.   Rural development programmes are often underfunded and understaffed.   Technology,
trained personnel and R and D institutions do not adequately deal
with the problems of the rural sector.   Credit is insufficiently
available.   And, where these resources are available in the rural
areas, women have severely limited access to them.

The studies indicate three ways in which the general lack
of resources invested in rural development places women in a
particularly disadvantaged position vis-à-vis access to inputs,
improved technology, credit, etc.   In all of Africa, there are very
few institutions that are capable of identifying the needs of and
carrying out research on the rural production process.   Stevens
and Tadesse both document this shortage.   Stevens also documents

the lack of technical institutions capable of planning effective
programmes and the lack of intermediate institutions to reach the
rural people and transmit information about technology and needs.

In general, although these studies describe women living and
working under grim conditions, they are not without prospects for the
women's future participation in the growth and improvement of the
rural communities.   Repeatedly, they demonstrate women's ability
to overcome the limitations imposed on them and to improve their
standards of living.   The greatest strides we find are where rural
women themselves have been involved in the design of programmes and
the programmes have encompassed social, economic, cultural and
political aspects of the women's roles.   However, another finding
that places doubt on the ease with which women can be expected to
partake in the design of rural development programmes is that one
of the obstacles to women's participation is attitudinal, including
the women's sense of their own limitations, both of activities and
of authority.

In the area of improved technologies, some substantial developments have occurred, especially where women have been involved in
the design stage.   In these cases, the new technologies have proven
to be better adapted to the needs of the rural population, and have
received much wider acceptance than in the (common) instances where
women have been excluded from planning and design.   These
technologies have had the effects of freeing women from time and
energy constraints, where they have been effective, thereby allowing
them to pursue income-generating activities, activities that
increase their human capital and their depleted human energy.
Some women have been given the additional opportunity to produce a
product for the market through the introduction of a new technology.
Integrated or "packaged" assistance, including training, new
technologies and the provision of credit to allow the women to afford
the new inputs and machines, has also proven to be more effective than
lone improvements in technologies.   An additional advantage to
co-ordinated assistance is the consideration of the social and cultural,
as well as economic and technical problems with the introduction of
new technologies, for these latter can be quite difficult to overcome
without work on a social level, as Date-Bah documents.

Very few of the new economic activities that rural women have
been able to engage in and that have proved successful in increasing
their incomes, standards of living and sense of their own abilities,

according to these studies, have been initiated by outside agents.
Externally planned activities and programmes tend to be poorly
suited to the women's needs, poorly suited to the social and economic
climates in which the women live and often sloppily and incompletely
executed.   However, a number of successful activities have been
initiated by the women themselves.   In this sample, all of them
revolve around women's traditional tasks and activities, such as
handicrafts and food production.   Although they have not yet allowed
women to break out of their traditional areas, they have moved women
successfully into production for the market.   In addition, the
organisation, initiative and sometimes solidarity the women display
in these examples clearly demonstrate their self-reliance and ability
to meet new challenges.   The spectrum of these activities runs from
petty trade, under radically different conditions, to production of
agricultural and traditional products for the market.

Petty traders in Nene's study from South Africa perform their
marketing activities out of desperation in an environment that gives
them no encouragement.   This activity is not new among the women, but
has been intensifying as poverty spreads and more women lose access
to land and to other sources of income and subsistence.   These women
work out of the need to survive and support their families.
With one significant exception, they work individually, and there is
little attempt to co-operate and organise themselves.   Each woman
sees trade as the only solution to her needs, and there is little
understanding revealed of underlying reasons for the common needs of the
women.   Under the present economic, social and political situation,
the author sees little chance for improvement of the women's working
conditions in South Africa but there is a great deal of work that can
be done to aid the women and to gradually weaken some specific constraints imposed on them by the regime.

Petty traders among the Moslem Hausa women in Longhurst's study
work under entirely different conditions and needs.   By and large,
they are better off women who are pursuing trade to supplement their
independent income, and their needs are not as immediate as those of
the South African women, nor is the environment as hostile.   Many of
these women carry out trade activities from seclusion, utilising the
labour of their children and occasionally husbands to make contacts
that are forbidden to them.   In addition, many of them take advantage
of indigenous credit structures, a credit society and the practice of
taking out formal loans from their husbands in order to finance some
larger trading ventures.   Their ingenuity and initiative in this
respect are remarkable, and the fact that they are able to trade as

they do is a strong indication of their ability to act independently
and productively in their socio-economic environment. However, it is
notable that these women seem not to have taken action to overcome
their seclusion, which imposes a ceiling on their ability to participate in trade.

In the Ivory Coast, Traoré finds a group of women engaged in
the production of attiéké, a traditional food. As with both of
the above examples, the women display considerable ingenuity and
fortitude in continuing their activities despite obstacles and
difficult conditions. They are hampered by serious constraints:
lack of land, lack of resources, problems with marketing and a
sexual division of labour that places responsibility for land clearing
on men. However, these women are slowly beginning to challenge
these constraints and move into new areas. They are beginning to
deal with the marketing of their own product and to tackle the
marketing problems. The tone of the paper is extremely positive
toward the initiative they have already taken, and the hope is
there that they will be able to carry their experience and initiative
beyond the simple, small-scale, labour-intensive production process
they currently utilise.

Similar problems have been encountered by women who attempt to
produce and market fruits, vegetables and dairy products on a small
scale in Senegal (Ba et al). Although several women have been
able to earn a minor income through these activities, the majority
suffer from severe time constraints (partially due to the fact that
they must work their husbands' lands before working their own), and
land constraints (as land tenure systems normally only allot land to
men, who are responsible for sharing it with their wives but do not
always turn over full responsibility and authority to them). They
also have problems with water shortage and transportation. The
study is very clear on the magnitude of these problems and the women's
inability so far to overcome them.

In Nigeria, Akande describes the activities of a number of
different kinds of women's groups - religious, cultural, age cohort,
co-operatives, credit societies, etc. She finds that many of these
have been able to initiate their own projects to enrich their
communities and improve the conditions of their own lives. An
unusual example is of women utilising their talents and skill at
traditional arts to set up a cultural dance performance in their
village, with the purpose of raising money for a new school.

The women invited the men and the people of the neighbouring villages to this benefit performance and succeeded in raising the needed money.   Although this approach has extremely limited potential to improve conditions in rural areas on a large scale, it certainly demonstrates an ability to organise, identify group needs and take action.   This is the ability that is all too often over-looked and swept aside in development planning by outside agents.

The kind of reliance on indigenous institutions, whether they be credit, cultural or agricultural institutions, that many of these examples demonstrate, has allowed women to make some headway in the process of rural development.   These institutions have the advantage of prior existence, and the women are not forced to go through a struggle to create them.   However, in other cases, new organisations and institutions have also been useful and effective. Women have repeatedly proven themselves able to form such new institutions when they are given the opportunity and they perceive the need.   Rural development programmes should recognise this ability and utilise the existing organisations as well as women's own initiative and enthusiasm.

Large-scale women's organisations, national ministries or branches of ministries, national organisations and international institutions can have a useful role in promoting women's participation, but these must be careful not to fall into the same pitfalls that external planners do.   They are often no more aware of the conditions under which the women live and work, and there is danger in the pretence of understanding.   Ba et al discuss the short-comings of such an organisation in Senegal.

Finally, Dhamija brings up the possibility of large-scale women's research, training and dissemination institutions.   She points out some of the problems such an organisation faces, and some of the measures it can take to overcome those problems.   She offers some positive examples of organisations and the ways in which they have been able to promote alternatives to agriculture for women who can no longer earn an acceptable living from it.

Chapter 1

STUDIES ON RURAL WOMEN IN AFRICA: AN OVERVIEW
by
Zenebeworke Tadesse

Introduction

The international economy and some limitations on women's participation in rural development

Agriculture is indoubtedly the principal form of production
in Africa and, contrary to the accounts of existing census data,
women make up a large proportion of the agricultural labour force.
Any study of the agricultural production process, if it were to be
accurate and comprehensive, would have to include a systematic
examination of the division of labour by sex. To the extent that
most studies on poverty and underdevelopment fail to take into
consideration that division of labour, and that most policy
implications are drawn from such incomplete studies, rural development programmes in Africa have failed to address effectively an
important cause of low productivity.

One should hasten to add that the mere inclusion of the sexual
division of labour would not solve these structural problems.
A descriptive addition of the division of labour or an exclusive
focus on women's role without analysing the overall determinants
of agricultural transformation and the resultant changes and/or
continuity of the pre-existing divisions of labour would only
lead to faulty conclusions and naive or harmful policy recommendations
recommendations.

The colonial intrusion and subsequent transformations of
rural Africa have resulted in a breakdown of the pre-existing social
structures and methods of production. What is more, the different
phases of African history - the slave trade, colonialism and the
ongoing processes of export promotion and import substitution
represent the various ways in which Africa was "integrated" into the
world economy.

All these processes have had profound impacts on agricultural
production and consequently on the relations of production and
reproduction. The most significant change in agriculture is the
growth of commercial agriculture, where priority is given to the

production of cash crops for export and urban markets.   The
agricultural production is subject to the vagaries of world market
prices and demand on the one hand, and to the rapid growth of the
urban population on the other.

However, since most fertile land and institutional support is
dedicated to the development of export crops, local production has
not been able to meet the growing local demand for agricultural
products.   The cumulative result of the scenario is that almost all
African countries have been forced to import food products in
addition to other commodities.

Consistent with the logic of capital accumulation, production of
cash crops has greatly changed the value, ownership and control of
land, the methods of production and the division of labour by sex.
The most significant of these changes has been the process of social
differentiation set in motion by the creation of the markets for
land and labour, which have led to a growing trend of land concentra-
tion in a few hands along with excessive land fragmentation in order
to accommodate the new high person-to-land ratio, and to the replacement of the traditional system of communal and reciprocal labour by
a more impersonal labour paid in kind or increasingly in cash by
the job or by the day.   Each of these processes has had differential
impacts on men and women, and it is precisely the study of the nature
of these different impacts that the contribution of research on rural
women should be.

The social implications of cash crop production are uneven and
reflect different forms of relations of production, diverse forms
of land tenure and varying processes of production.   In fact
certain pre-existing forms of production are preserved and one finds
these pre-existing forms of production next to the most modern
agricultural projects.

However, a closer examination of these forms would indicate
substantive transformations taking place beneath what appears as
"traditional".

Historically, at a simple level of description, "traditional"
implied self-sufficient households whose production was primarily
geared towards subsistence farming using simple tools and having
very little to do with cash transactions.   "Modernisation" and
"agricultural development" are concepts that are often used inter-
changeably and are meant to describe regions and households which

are mainly geared towards production for the market and characterised
by relatively large holdings, increased use of cash inputs,
specialisation of roles and increased productivity of labour.
Increasing commoditisation in agricultural production has altered
the primary purpose of cultivation to that of producing surplus
to sell rather than to consume, and has created the need to
supplement farm income by engaging in other income generating
activities even for the "traditional" sector.   The differences are
seen in the volume, types of crops sold and the income generating
activities chosen.

Apart from the problem of lack of conceptual clarity within the
modernisation literature, the problem of the choice of the unit
of analysis emerges, i.e. farmer or household whose decision-making
will be affected by the development of capitalism in agriculture.
The image of males as the sole and universal farmer juxtaposed to
that of women as primarily housewives relegated only to "housework"
which might or might not include susbsistence farming, obscures
women's actual role in production, the multiplicity of tasks that
housework denotes in a rural household and reproductive tasks on
a daily and generational basis.   The concept of rural development,
on the other hand, encompasses a variety of planned agricultural
changes ranging from large commercial farming which hire both
permanent and seasonal labour and extension programmes for individual
farm households.   With the exception of the large highly mechanised
farms, the implementation of these changes is premised on the
availability of unremunerated family labour.   Rural women and children
children participate in many apsects of the labour process but do
not control the final product.   They are not really "integrated".
Not every member in the household benefits equally from the process.

With the primary aim of producing for the international or urban
market, the process entails varying degrees of changes in the
cropping pattern, maximum use of land, use of purchased inputs,
demand of more labour and the use of machinery, technical changes
which maintain and intensify the hierarchisation of sex roles.

Research on women's roles
in rural development

Thus far, research has tended to obscure the sexual division of
labour and the socio-economy underlying the production process.
Recently, however, studies have begun to consider the special roles

men and women play in different stages of development. Boserup
was the first to focus on the relationship between women's roles
and economic development, documenting the ties between certain land
use patterns and agricultural techniques, and the sexual division
of labour. She characterised the African agricultural system as
the female farming system par excellence. Female farming systems
are to be found where there is an abundance of land relative to
population and, therefore, long fallow cultivation using digging
sticks or hoes as tools. As Africa is the region where shifting
cultivation and the hoe are predominant, the division of labour
is such that men clear the land for cultivation while women carry
out the actual cultivation of food crops for subsistence.

Boserup's typology places plough agriculture in a later stage of
development, and associates with it a decline in the participation
of women in agriculture. A related idea is that men produce cash
crops, while women are responsible for the annual food crop.
Colonialism and present day agricultural experts have exacerbated
the tendency for cash crop production to be in male hands because
of the European view that farming is a "male" occupation. As a
result, women's predominant role in African agriculture has been
ignored and rural women have lost their right to land due to land
reforms introduced by European administrators. Consequently, women
are rarely involved in the development process either as participants
or beneficiaries, as experts fail to assign any roles for women in
programmes of training for agricultural modernisation and other
development projects. Hence, an urgent call for the integration
of women in development.

Although Boserup's work has been criticised for failing to
recognise that women have, indeed, been integrated into the rural
modernisation programmes as unpaid and unrecognised familial and
subsistence labourers, her work has sparked a considerable amount
of debate and empirical research. Now there is a fair sized and
growing body of knowledge on the subject of women's contribution to
the production process.

Women's role in the rural economy

All over Africa, women play a central role in food production
and preparation. An estimate of the percentage of the labour
associated with each task involved in food production points out
that women contribute 70 per cent of the labour in food production,

while they are solely responsible for food processing.   The sexual
division of labour in food production is both task and crop specific.
Men are primarly involved in land clearing, grow perennial crops,
provide meat, raise larger animals, while women are responsible for
hoeing, planting, thinning and weeding, caring for the small
domestic animals.   In addition, women are responsible for the time-
consuming and numerous tasks associated with the preservation and
preparation of food.   Given the nature of rural underdevelopment in
Africa, these tasks can take up to four times as long as all the work
hours spent on the cultivation of the crop.   In almost all cases,
women are responsible for providing most of the food consumption
needs of the family.

The growth of cash cropping, which has accompanied the spread
of the cash economy into rural Africa has had significant effects on
the sexual division of labour and the resources available to men and
women.   Women are being forced to sell some of their surplus, spend
more time on their husbands' cash crops and engage in a variety of
income-generating activities.   The fragmentation of land, the
increasing population density and the tendency toward male out-
migration further increases the women's workload.   Women, thus,
begin to shift their cropping patterns toward crops with higher
yields per acre and per woman-day and away from more nutritious but
more time-consuming crops.

Agricultural modernisation

Agricultural modernisation programmes in Africa have tended to
be based on large-scale mechanisation, irrigation of previously
unirrigated areas and cash cropping.   Rather than addressing the
problems of most of the rural women, they have tended to increase the
women's workload.   Rarely are attempts made to introduce labour-
saving devices for the women's use in tasks that are traditionally
theirs.   Thus, women must work much harder if they are to participate in the programmes or they must take over their husbands'
chores, while the men participate in the modernisation programmes.
Women have been stuck with the so-called "dual burden" of household
and reproductive work as well as "productive" work.

Rural development programmes have also failed to provide women
with sources of income.   In some cases, they have even deprived
them of income-generating activities engaged in prior to the
development programmes.   Traditional female activities have, in some

places, been mechanised and turned over to men, or the women have
been unable to obtain the necessary raw materials.   Rural women are
often dispossessed from their land during agricultural modernisation
programmes that depend on the consolidation of smallholdings.
Besides depriving women of the land necessary for their subsistence,
this reinforces the bias against women in the allocation of credit.
Without any collateral, which is usually land in rural Africa, women
are considered ineligible for most credit-extension programmes.

Gender is not the only limitation to participation in rural
development schemes.   Many people are also restricted in their
participation on the basis of their class, or the region they come
from.   The process of social differentiation has taken place in
varied ways in different regions throughout Africa, and it has
affected the households' abilities to command resources to varying
degrees.   Women, however, are often at the bottom of the ladder in
terms of the resources at their disposal, as they may be discriminated
against on the basis of their sex as well as their class or regional
background.   This problem of unequal channelling of resources has
hurt entire populations, for it has substantially lowered the
productivity of the agriçultural sector.

Impact of male migration on women's work

The uneven regional development and the development of
commercialisation in agriculture have led to the creation of a
non-agricultural labour market to which men are very often the
first ones to migrate.   The result has been a change in the sexual
division of labour as tasks regarded as that of males are, by
necessity, taken over by women.   In some regions women have been
left as the sole agriculturalists, increasing their responsibility
for family maintenance and reproduction.

Women's organisations

Women's organisations have a tremendous variety of functions
across Africa.   There are formal nation-wide organisations, credit
organisations, non-governmental organisations, international
organisations, national machineries and informational organisations.   The class composition of these organisations plays
an important role in the way they perceive their roles.
Organisations of upper-class women tend to see their function as
social.   Either they are purely for the social pleasure of the
women involved, or they are welfare oriented.   Rural women's
organisations tend to be oriented more toward self-help programmes.

Before assigning these organisations a central role in the integration of women into rural development programmes, it is important to notice that the constituency of the organisation makes a tremendous difference in its access to policy-making mechanisms. The social organisations of the upper and middle-class women, often urban based, while they have the greatest access to state and policy instruments, do not represent the needs and interests of the majority of women. Their attempts at social change, rather than aiding the rural women in meaningful ways, sometimes even divert resources and attention from their most basic needs and place more obstacles in the way of their participation in rural development.

In spite of these contradictory pressures, rural women are often receptive to beneficial forms of collective action. If based on the actual needs of the majority of rural women, organisations can provide an arena for women's struggle for survival, and act as networks of useful information. Through their potential for consciousness-raising, they can challenge existing stereotypes that reproduce women's subordination.

BIBLIOGRAPHY

Abbott, S.: A seven country survey on the roles of women in rural development. Report for USAID Development Alternative Inc. (Washington, DC), 1974.

Agarwal, B.: Agricultural modernisation and third world women: Pointers from the literature and an empirical analysis. (Geneva, ILO; mimeographed World Employment Programme research working paper; restricted), 1981.

Amin, S.: Accumulation on a world scale: a critique of the theory of underdevelopment (New York, Monthly Review Press), 1974.

Bates, R.H.; Lofchies, M.F.: Agricultural development in Africa: Issues of public policy (New York, Praeger), 1980.

Beneria L., Sen, G.: Accumulation, reproduction and women's role in economic development: Boserup revisited. Paper presented at Burg Weinstein Symposium No. 85, 1980.

Boserup, E.: The conditions of agricultural growth (Chicago, Aldine Publishing Co:), 1965.

Brain, J.: "Less than second-class: women in rural settlement schemes in Tanzania", in Women in Africa (Stanford, California, Stanford University Press), 1976.

Bukh, J.: The village women in Ghana (Uppsala, Scandinavian Institute of African Studies), 1979.

Deere, C.D. et al.: Class and historical analysis for the study of women and economic change. Paper presented for the role of women and demographic change research programme (Geneva, ILO), 1979.

De Vellenza, D.: "Differentiation among women farmers in two rural areas in Ghana", in Labour and Society, Vol. 2, No. 2, 1977.

Edholm, F. et al.: "Conceptualizing women" in Critique of Anthropology, 9:10 Vol. 3, pp. 101-130, 1972.

Fedman and Lawrence: Global project on the social and economic implications of large-scale introduction of new varieties of food grains: Africa report (Geneva, United Nations Research Institute for Social Development), 1975.

Hanger and Morris: "Women and the household economy". Chambers and Morris (eds.), in An Irrigated Rice Settlement in Kenya, (Munich, Weltforum Verlag), 1973.

Hoskins, M.: Income generating activities with women's participation: a re-examination of goals and issues (AID OTR/147-80-76), 1980.

Jellicoe, M.S.: Indigenous savings associations and the mobilisation of domestic savings (Addis Ababa), 1963.

Lele, U.: The design of rural development: lessons from Africa
     (Baltimore, Hopkins University Press), 1975.

McLoughlin, P.: African food production systems (Baltimore,
     Hopkins University Press), 1970.

Meillassoux, C.: "The social organisation of the peasantry", in
     Journal of peasant studies. 1(1), 81-90, 1973.

Meuller, M.: "Women and men power and powerlessness in Lesotho"
     in Signs, 1977.

Ministry of Agriculture: Mahangatsha RBA. Survey results and
     analysis. 1976/77 Farm Management Survey Report No. 3,
     Monitoring and Evaluation Unit, 1978.

Monstead, M.: Women's groups in rural Kenya and their role in
     development. CDR Papar A/78/2 (Copenhagen), 1978.

Muntemba, M.: "The underdevelopment of peasant agriculture in
     Zambia", in Journal of Southern African Studies, Vol. 5,
     No. 1, 58-85, 1978.

Sanday, P.: "Female Status in the Public Domain", in Women,
     culture and society (Stanford, Stanford University Press), 1974.

Savane, M.A.: Les Femmes africaines dans le problématique du
     développement. Paper presented to the Seminar on Africa and
     the Future (Dakar), 1977.

Spencer, D.: African women in agricultural development: a case
     study in Sierra Leone. (East Lansing, Dept. of Agricultural
     Economics, Michigan State University), 1976.

Staudt, K.: "Agricultural productivity gaps: a case study of
     male preference in government policy implementation" in
     Development and Change, Vol. 9, No. 3, pp. 439-57, 1978.

Tadesse, Z.: An overview on women's organisations in Africa:
     The case of Ethiopia, Mozambique and Tanzania. Paper
     presented at the 9th World Congress of Sociology (Uppsala), 1978.

UN/ECA/ATRCW: The role of women in population dynamics, related
     to food and agriculture and rural development in Africa.
     (ECA/FAO Women's Programme Unit, Addis Ababa) 1974.

UN/ECA/ATRCW: "Women and national development in African countries:
     some profound contradictions", in African Studies Review,
     XVIII, 3, 1975.

UN/ECA/ATRCW: The role of women in African development, p. 61.

US Agency for International Development: A seven-country survey
     on the role of women in rural development. A report prepared
     for the AID under Development Alternatives Inc. (Washington, DC),
     1979.

Wallerstein, I.: "Three stages of African involvement in the
     world economy", in The political economy of contemporary Africa.
     (Sage Publication, pp. 30-57, 1976.

Wild, J.C.: Experiences with agricultural development in tropical
     Africa, 2 vols. (Baltimore, J. Hopkins Press), 1967.

Chapter 2

INCOME-GENERATING ACTIVITIES FOR RURAL WOMEN IN AFRICA: SOME SUCCESSES AND FAILURES

by

Jasleen Dhamija

The situation of African women in the employment sector is not encouraging. Agriculture accounts for 72 per cent of women's participation in the labour force, and that figure is rising. However, agricultural resources cannot continue to absorb the new entrants into the sector, and even those already employed do not have full productive employment. The returns to the new entrants will not be sufficient to support them.

It is, therefore, imperative to develop policies for the training of women in other sectors. These policies could depend on the upgrading of traditional skills through the introduction of new technologies and processes, the training of new skills, and the diversification of traditional skills.

The majority of the population in Africa lives in rural areas, and engages in agricultural production. Many of these people live on the edge of poverty, and to them a square meal is a luxury. Cash, which is needed for such basic needs as salt and oil, is scarce, and the government services, such as welfare and health, do not reach the rural people. No one asks how useful it is to instruct these people in nutritious diet preparation for children when they cannot give their children one square meal a day. Home economists, who teach the importance of washing children and clothes with soap, often do not realise that rural women cannot afford to buy soap, and thus many of the training programmes in home economics are useless.

There is very little communication between the rural people and those who design rural development policy, but when a field worker or a workshop leader does reach out to these people, they can spell out their needs very clearly. In addition, policy-makers are not aware of the fact that extension programmes rarely reach the poorest rural families, neither men nor women. Landless and rural non-farm families have almost no contact with government institutions, and agricultural modernisation programmes completely overlook them. Of this group, it is the women who bear the brunt of the poverty, for it is their responsibility to see that there is food, to prepare it and to supply all the needs of the family.

Often male out-migration takes place among this group of families, and women are left by themselves and must perform all their own household tasks and support their families as head of the household. They take the responsibility of providing not only for the nuclear family but also the extended family and yet the data often do not reflect this situation for the head of the household still remains the man who may have not been an effective head of household for a decade or so.

The gap between rural and urban standards of living is growing, and in the rural areas the number of landless people is also growing. Priority has to be given to the development of agriculture, but there is also need to emphasise the development of rural non-farm activities.

Although women have always participated in all levels of production in Africa, the process of development is leaving them out. New technologies are invariably directed toward men, and where women get to participate in their use, the benefits almost always accrue to men. A very small per cent of women, compared with men, have access to informal agricultural training or agricultural co-operatives. Although women have traditionally been responsible for food preparation, as soon as a new mechanised process is introduced, it is handed over to men.

An example of discrimination against women can be seen at M'bour (Senegal), where a number of women had been entrepreneurs in a fish-processing centre that employed men as wage workers. The Government introduced ovens for smoking the fish and handed them over to men. When asked why this had occurred, the local authorities answered that the women preferred to work in the open air. Now the women's association of 800 women is collecting funds to build their own ovens and has asked for assistence. However, the authorities see their organisation as exploitative and are planning to organise co-operatives of fishermen to do their own processing, although it is known that the fishermen cannot do both their own fishing and processing. What is likely to happen is that businessmen will gain control of the government-assisted co-operative and use the women as cheap labour.

Even in the female dominated markets, rather than introducing judicious controls and education to draw on the talent of the women in building up distribution systems, the female contribution is being undermined by the development policies.

The industrialisation programmes which lead to urbanisation often take place at the expense of the women. In all areas and all industries, women are employed as unskilled workers only. The pre-vocational and vocational training programmes are either directed only toward men, or the type of subjects taught to the women do not give them the necessary qualifications for skilled or supervisory positions. It would not be correct to say that women do not take available opportunities, for where women are encouraged, they do take the initiative and may even go beyond the targeted training openings directed toward them. If women are seen as active participants in the economy of a country, and if they are given opportunities for entry into areas such as farming, industry, trading and management, they will utilise them. But if planners see the African women as cooks, housekeepers, child bearers and sex objects, then the services and resources as well as social attitudes extended to them will be directed toward that end, and the society will not benefit from their productive capacity.

A great deal of harm done to the African women stems from the lack of understanding of the women's role by regional planners, international experts and even national planners whose training and points of reference are based on the status of women in Europe, the Middle East and South Asia. They fail to realise the dominant role that women play in the rural economy, and the new planning strategies are, therefore, not supportive of the women. One example of the effect of poor understanding is the land reforms, which have denied women the right to cultivate land they had previously depended on to support their families to feed their children. Now whole families are hungry as a result.

There is also an attitude among planners that women ought to be involved in the so-called feminine industries, such as handicrafts and household activities. These are labour-intensive and income-preserving, rather than income-generating activities. As soon as large-scale programmes based on new technologies can be set up to replace these activities, they become the domain of men.

We have to break out of the meaningless distinctions which have been created between skills associated with men and women. Why should women be denied access to areas of activities because of taboos that exist and are only meant for women? If we look at the broad spectrum of activities performed by women in Africa, salt processing and mining, charcoal manufacture, metal working, wood working, etc. we cannot lay down any hard and fast rules concerning women's activities and men's.   The only rule appears to be that when a new technology is introduced, which means upgraded skills and higher returns, it is men who take over.   This appears to be the case even in historical perspective.

We who are involved in development programmes are not blameless, for we see a woman in a stereotyped role and we think only in terms of alleviating her immediate situation by the introduction of a tool here or a skill there.   One programme that has tried to break these stereotypes is the Handicrafts and Small-Scale Industries Unit, a joint ILO/ECA/SIDA project in the African Training and Research Centre for Women (ATRCW), Addis Ababa.   This programme tried to create an awareness among the policy-makers, women's organisations and existing national institutions of the need for reorienting the programmes for women toward income-generating activities, rather than income-preserving activities.   It also tried to strengthen the existing women's programmes and institutions by orienting their activities to changing socio-economic needs, and by linking/integrating them with other institutions and governmental departments so that they could utilise the technical and institutional structures already developed at the regional and national levels.

This was undertaken through training conducted by internships and fellowships, through workshops and seminars, through consultancy services offered to governments, through research and studies, preparation of teaching materials and publications, as well as by setting up pilot projects which had demonstrational value. Such pilot projects included programmes in the development of garment-making industries, manufacture of indigenous construction materials through diversification of pottery skills, training of women in non-traditional skills in electronics, machine tools, etc.

For the effective development of women's participation in rural industries and their entry into the modern sector, it is necessary to develop an integrated approach to women's access to education, technical innovation, vocational training, credit and institutional support.   In addition to this, there is the need for the development of infrastructure in the rural areas to relieve women from the chores which occupy them and prevent their full participation in more remunerative activities.

Chapter 3

TECHNOLOGIES FOR RURAL WOMEN'S ACTIVITIES:
PROBLEMS AND PROSPECTS IN SIERRA LEONE

by

Yvette Stevens

Introduction

Rural women in Sierra Leone are essential participants in the
economy.   Their daily work, often unpaid and unrecognised, makes a
major contribution toward the survival of the population, yet programmes in rural development have largely bypassed them.   Most programmes do not take their special needs and burdens into account,
focusing instead on raising the output and efficiency of other
sectors.   Benefits from increased output do not, generally, reach
the women, and often the programmes have a destructive, rather than
benign effect on the amount and quality of women's work.   Their
work, often invisible to planners, tends to become heavier as more
and more resources are withdrawn for use in the development programmes.

This study examines the kinds of work women do and the pressures
they perform under.   It then explores some important criteria for
the successful adoption of improved technologies that would focus on
women's work.   Finally, making use of those criteria, the author
makes her own suggestions on areas in which the development and
dissemination of improved technologies would be of tremendous value
to those women and the rural economy as a whole.

The vast majority of Sierra Leone's population is rural dwelling
and engages in agricultural activities for subsistence.   Rice is
the staple crop; it is grown both in the upland region, where productivity is very low, and in the swampy regions, where productivity
is more than twice as high.   The low-productivity upland regions,
however, account for more than 1/2 the rice produced (64 per cent).
Although Sierra Leone used to be entirely self-sufficient in rice
production, indeed, she used to export rice, the growth of the
diamond mining industry in the late fifties placed such a drain on
the rural male population, that Sierra Leone now depends on imported
rice.   The continued trend of rural/urban migration has aggravated
this drain.   Other important crops are cassava, sorghum, groundnuts,
sweet potatoes and vegetables.   Water supply is a basic problem as

as in many other developing countries; but in contrast to many African countries Sierra Leone possesses vast hydro resources, although the full potential has yet to be assessed. The more prevalent land tenure system is communal ownership. A survey in 1970 showed that only 6 per cent of the agricultural holdings were held by women; however, where rice lands are allotted to women, the use of the rice produced is controlled by the males.

Within the rural production process, there is a strict division of labour that reflects the prevailing ideology towards women. Women are expected to be under male supervision in everything they do. In some areas a woman is not supposed to live without the "care and protection" of a man and thus the traditional division of labour is not designed to make them self-sufficient. Agriculture is usually a co-operative venture between the men and women in a family. Even so, it can absorb up to eight or nine hours a day of the woman's time during peak periods in rice farming. It should be noted that the provision of rice for the family is the responsibility of the men. Agriculture is typically women's primary occupation, but not their only one. Women are also responsible for food processing, child care and all the household chores, such as water and firewood gathering. In some areas, women also engage in cotton farming or petty trading to bring in some additional cash.

The continued male rural/urban migration trend has had a particularly hard effect on these rural women. They are now responsible not only for the chores that are traditionally theirs, but also for the entire agricultural process. Often the resources available to the woman living alone are less than those she would have access to were her husband living with her.

Rural technologies currently in use
by rural women

The Government of Sierra Leone has recognised the plight of the rural people with regard to their shortage of food and water. They have begun a number of projects to alleviate some of these problems. Those projects, however, have not, by and large, been aimed at the rural women, and they have done little to improve the efficiency and quality of the numerous tasks the women have to perform. A survey of some of these tasks and the traditional technologies utilised is sufficient to demonstrate that there is a great deal of room for improvement.

Cooking is most commonly done using the "three stone method".
A pot is balanced on top of three stones, arranged in a triangle,
and a fire is lit beneath it.   To the rural women this method has
the advantage that cooking can be done sitting down.   In addition,
the ash produced as a by-product has several household uses, and
the fuel, usually wood, is free or very cheap.   It is, however, a
very inefficient, unhealthy and dangerous method.   With small
children around, there are frequent burn accidents; a great deal of
heat is lost, and when cooking is done indoors, the whole family must
breathe the smoke.

Some of these wealthier families use a variety of different
methods, but these are not available to the majority of people.
Often they require a capital investment well beyond the means of the
majority (improved charcoal stoves, for example), or they utilise
an expensive fuel, such as kerosene.

Water collection, as in many other African countries, is a
major problem.   Available water is often contaminated.   When
underground water is accessible, hand-dug open wells are available
and water is pulled up by ropes tied to buckets.   There have been
some projects on the installation of pumps but problems with the
frequent replacement of cylinders have undermined their effect.
When underground water is not easily accessible, water is fetched
from rivers and streams.   In many areas, women must walk for miles
to find it, and then carry it back to their homes on their heads.
This must be done frequently, for even when such sources as rain
water are easily available, there is a general lack of sufficient
or hygienic storage facilities.

Food preservation involves both sun drying of such products as
grains, vegetables, herbs, salted fish and smoking of fish.   Both
of these methods are time consuming, unhygienic and inefficient.
Often drying is incomplete, resulting in a high degree of spoilage
and much of the protein content is destroyed.

Both the production and the processing of rice are difficult
and inefficient with the traditional tools and technologies.   In
particular, the rice must be par-boiled before removing the husks.
With the traditional cooking methods, this is an especially labour-
intensive and inefficient step.

Other types of food processing that are commonly practised are
palm oil and palm kernel oil extraction.   Boiling and fermentation
are the two traditional methods used although with a low technical

efficiency.   Oil mills have been introduced in Sierra Leone at
different times in the past, but most of these were not successful,
because of their failure to take account of the traditional economics
of palm oil production.   People simply stopped selling the nuts to
the mill, because, in their eyes, it made more financial sense for
them to process the nuts on their own.   The Government has invested
in a few palm oil mills of its own, which are associated with oil
palm plantations.   These are limited scale, pilot projects,
however, and their success has yet to be determined.

The most successful technological improvements in palm oil
processing have been the few simple and light screw presses that
have found their way into Sierra Leone by chance.

Cassava, sesame seeds, coconuts, beans, groundnuts and maize
are all processed, using traditional methods, into goods that are
consumed or sold.   Many of these methods involve grating, pounding
with a mortar and pestle, grinding between two stones, boiling and
drying, all difficult, inefficient and often unhygienic processes.

Soap making, shallow water fishing and handicrafts are all
specialised women's tasks that may contribute directly to the household's consumption or income.   Tie-dying (gara) has an important
potential as a source on income.   However, the use of traditional,
natural dyes, especially indigo, is laborious and often leaves un-
pleasant odors in the fabric.   The range of colours available is
limited and colourfastness is difficult to ensure.   Synthetic dyes
have become readily available and extensively used.   They eliminate
the problems associated with the natural dyes and are much easier to
use.   However, their price has tripled in the last few years, and
many traditional tie-dyers have been forced out of business.

Criteria for adoption of new rural technologies

Given the conditions under which most rural production takes
place, and utilising the few examples of technologies that did or
did not work, some criteria can be set forth by which to identify
and evaluate potential technological improvements.   The evaluation
of new rural technologies falls into three categories: availability,
practicality and profitability.   Under each of these, a number of
questions must be considered.

Availability: Is the technology freely obtainable in the market (assuming the target group knows of its existence)? Can the woman afford to buy it, either directly or through an available credit scheme? Can it be purchased by collective effort? Can the woman afford to pay for its use?

Practicality: Does the technology disrupt prevailing social, cultural and religious life or blend with it? Can it be operated by the women themselves? Is it convenient for the women to use? Can it be easily maintained and repaired?

Profitability: Is time, labour or money saved by the new technology? Does it provide more income? Are there marketing problems?

To ensure that the proper conditions are met under each of these areas, a number of steps will have to be taken. Research and development institutions will have to focus on cutting down costs of their final products through the use of locally produced material, mass production or overall simplicity of materials and production process. Where the basic components (such as steel and aluminium sheets and rods, nails, rivets, etc.) are not produced locally, the Government should ensure their availability at a reasonable price by subsidising imports. Extension work, to inform women of the innovations and give advice, should be intensified, and mass media should be exploited wherever possible.

In the area of practicality, socio-economic studies must be performed in order to identify the areas in which reform is most urgently needed and would be most effective. Studies of existing technologies also allow the identification of those ones which are already efficient and not possible to improve on at a reasonable cost. Findings on the type of labour employed, the customs, traditions and religious beliefs must be incorporated in the design stage. The local people must be consulted at all stages of design and production, as this has proven to increase the relevance and acceptability of the final product. These studies must enable the designer to assess the capabilities of local expertise and the possibility of maintenance and repair.

Finally, to ensure that the technology will prove profitable, the designer must be certain that his method is truly an improvement in performance. For income-generating activities, the economist must assess the market for the finished product, its ability to absorb the product and give a profitable rate of return. In the case of time-saving devices, there must be adequate incentive to save time. Perhaps income-generating activities could be set up in the time no longer devoted to farming and household chores. Finally, infrastructural facilities for marketing and supporting the new facilities must be made available at an affordable cost, utilising locally available resources where possible.

Evaluating the improved technologies already developed and introduced by the R&D institutions according to these criteria, this study finds that they do not meet the conditions required for wide-spread use. Most of them are simply not available to women either because of their prohibitive cost or the lack of extension services targeted at women. R&D institutions themselves lack funds to undertake studies that would identify needs in the first place and to design appropriate technologies. There are few effective inter-mediate institutions between R&D facilities and villages. Thus, there is no channel through which information on needs, problems, or technology can flow, in either direction, and many promising tech-nologies never get beyond the testing stage. Credit in rural areas is hopelessly inadequate. It is mostly available to those who have the least need of it or at very high rates through tradi-tional sources.

Some suggested improved technologies

Although the situation and outlook for rural women seem pretty dismal thus far, there are some projects that have succeeded, and some prospects for the introduction of simple, cheap, available and effective technologies. New cooking stoves have potential to improve both the time and work efficiency of cooking. Raised cook-ing platforms could make food preparation more hygienic, removing the food from the dusty ground. A range of agricultural and indus-trial waste products could be explored as potential fuels.

Small-scale manual pumps, solar or hydropower pumps, wheel-barrows and carts for transporting water and cement storage jars are all underutilised but could be made available at a relatively minor cost. Water filters made of cheap local or imported materials would be simple to make and install, and would make a tremendous improvement in the over-all health of the rural communities.

Mechanisation of rice processing is expensive but brings great savings in time and energy. Small-scale machines that are cheaper, easier to transport and can be used in the household have also been developed and have great potential.

In the area of food drying and smoking a number of improvements have been made and introduced in pilot projects that meet all the criteria outlined above.

Finally, a range of small and large-scale shellers, mills and graters are available. The problem remains to adapt them to the specific situation and disseminate them among the population. Those tools and devices that serve the greatest number of purposes are the most effective, given the problems with transportation and lack of other essential storage and maintenance infrastructure. Attention could be given to combining the functions of some of these tools and devices.

It should also be noted here that the women of Sierra Leone have a tradition of organisations and group co-operation. These organisations can be extremely efficient in setting up and maintaining co-operative ventures. Rather than building a whole new set of institutions, these existing institutions could be exploited in the dissemination of information and technology.

Conclusion

The fact that simple, improved, acceptable technologies exist, but are not widely distributed points to a gap in the processing and passing on of information. This gap may have several causes: the shortage of funds for R&D institutions to both develop and disseminate technologies in co-operation with the rural population, the present insufficient manufacturing capability of those R&D institutions, the high cost of manufacturing, the general lack of rural credit and the information gap between what is available and what the rural women are aware of. The elimination of this gap is of primary importance to the 39 per cent of the population that is made up of rural women, who spend their days in endless toil in order to produce the basic life-sustaining necessities. That their problems are critical and need to be addressed directly must be recognised by the authorities. The improvement of their living standards can be achieved with new improved technologies. The first step, however, is to reorient development programmes toward their needs and to educate the women themselves to accept changes and improvements in their lives. Once these changes are made, technology packages incorporating women's tasks can begin to improve their situation.

BIBLIOGRAPHY

Ahmad, Z.: "The plight of rural women: Alternatives for action", in International Labour Review (Geneva, ILO, 1980), Vol. 119, No. 4.

Ahmed, I.: "Technological change and the condition of rural women: A preliminary assessment" (ILO WEP 2-22/WP 39, 1978).

Anwooner-Renner, M.: A visual geography of Sierra Leone (Evans Brothers Ltd., 1974).

Baron, C.: Technology, employment and basic needs in food processing in developing countries (Pergamon Press, 1980).

Bassey, M.W.: Report on Palm Oil Press Workshop (ECA/SL Government Palm Oil Project, 1979).

Bassey, M.W.: "Technical aspects in the implementation of appropriate technology - Role of the Faculty of Engineering, Fourah Bay College". Paper presented at the Workshop for Trainers and Planners on Village Technology for the Rural Family (Freetown, 1979).

Beoku-Betts, J.: "Western perceptions of African women in the 19th and early 20th centuries", Africana Research Bulletin (Institute of African Studies, University of Sierra Leone, Vol. VI, No. 4, 1976).

Bhaduri, A.: "Technological change and rural women - A conceptual analysis" (ILO WEP 2-22/WP 46, 1979).

Carr, M.: Appropriate technology and African women (ECA/SDP/ATRCW/VIGEN/78, 1978).

Carr, M.: "Technology and rural women in Africa" (ILO WEP 2-22/WP 61, 1980).

Chuta, E.: "The economics of gara (tie-dye) production in Sierra Leone, Africana Rural Economy Programme, Michigan State University, WP 25, 1978.

Chuta, E.: Growth and change in small-scale industry: Sierra Leone, 1974-80 (unpublished), 1980.

Cole, M.J. and Hamilton, D.: Indigenous technology in Sierra Leone (Sierra Leone Government/ECA/UNICEF Report, 1976).

Government of Sierra Leone: Statistical Bulletin, Vol. 17 (Central Statistics Office, 1970).

Government of Sierra Leone: Agricultural survey report (Ministry of Agriculture and Natural Resources, 1970).

Government of Sierra Leone: Statistical Bulletin, Vol. 19 (Central Statistics Office, 1971).

Government of Sierra Leone: Household surveys of the rural areas of the provinces, July 1969-January 1970 (Central Statistics Office, 1972).

Government of Sierra Leone: 1974/75-1978/79 Five-Year Plan (Ministry of Development and Economic Planning, 1974).

Government of Sierra Leone: Annual Statistical Digest (Central Statistics Office, 1976).

Government of Sierra Leone: Annual Statistical Digest (Central Statistics Office, 1977).

Government of Sierra Leone/UNCSTD: Report on Subregional Seminar (Freetown, July 1978).

Government of Sierra Leone: National nutrition survey report, 1978.

Government of Sierra Leone: Household surveys, 1980 (unpublished).

Government of Sierra Leone: Co-operative Department paper presented at the Workshop for Trainers and Planners on Village Technology for the Rural Family (Freetown, 1979).

Harrel Bond, B.E. and Rijnsdorp, U.: "The emergence of the 'stranger permit marriage' and other new forms of conjugal union in rural Sierra Leone", in Africana Research Bulletin, Vol. VI, No. 4 (Institute of African Studies, University of Sierra Leone).

ILO: Appropriate technology for employment creation in the food processing and drinks industries of developing countries (Geneva, 1978).

ILO: Women in rural development - Critical issues (Geneva, 1980).

Jackson, A.F.J.: "The potentials of indigenous and appropriate technology in national development", Report, UNCSTD Sub-regional Seminar (Freetown, 1978).

Jonston, R.: "Co-operatives and agricultural production in Sierra Leone", in Rural Africana (East Lansing, 1969).

Kaniki, M.: "Economical technology against technical efficiency in the palm oil industry of West Africa: Development and change", in SAGE (London and Beverly Hills, 1980), Vol. II, pp. 273-284.

Longhurst, R.: "Rural development planning and the sexual division of labour - A case study in the Moslem Hausa village in northern Nigeria" (ILO WEP 10/WP.10, 1980).

Loutfi, M.: Rural women: Unequal partners in development (ILO, Geneva, 1980).

MacCormack, C.: "The compound head - Structure and strategies", in Africana Research Bulletin, Vol. VI, No. 4, 1976 (Department of African Studies, University of Sierra Leone).

Nath, K. and Thomas, A.T.: Indicators of regional development, National Development Planning Paper, No. 11/39.

National Academy of Sciences, USA: Energy for rural development (Washington, DC, 1976).

Okelly, B.: Rural women: Their integration in development programmes and how simple intermediate technologies can help them (London, 1978).

Ottenburg, S.: "Artistic and sex roles in a Limba chiefdom" (unpublished), 1980.

Pilgrim, J.: "Social aspects of agricultural development in Sierra Leone - II technical development", in Sierra Leone Studies (Freetown, 1968).

Reish, I.: "Contribution of women to rural development with special emphasis on Africa", presented at Seminar on Problems in Rural Areas considering the Role of Radio in Development Process (1978).

Spencer, D.: "African women in agricultural development: A case study in Sierra Leone" (American Council of Education, OLC, 1976), Paper No. 9.

Spencer, D.: "Labour market organisation, wage rates and employment in the rural areas of Sierra Leone", in Labour and Society, 1979.

Thomas, K.: Keynote address, International Conference on Appropriate Technology in Rural Societies (Freetown, 1978).

Thomas, K.: "Collective responsibility for discovering Africa's vanished traditional techniques", paper presented at International Conference on Appropriate Technology in Rural Societies (Freetown, 1978).

UNICEF: Appropriate village technology for basic services (UNICEF/Kenya Government Village Technology Unit, Nairobi).

UNICEF: Simple technologies for rural women in Bangladesh (Bangladesh Women's Development Programme).

University of Sierra Leone/Sierra Leone Institution of Engineers, Summary Report, International Conference on Appropriate Technology in Rural Societies (Freetown, 1978).

Chapter 4

RURAL WOMEN, THEIR ACTIVITIES AND TECHNOLOGY
IN GHANA: AN OVERVIEW
by
Eugenia Date-Bah

This study focuses on the activities of rural women in Ghana,
the technologies they use in the performance of their daily tasks,
potential improvements in those technologies and limitations on
those improvements.   Beginning with an examination of the women's
activities, certain areas in need of improved technology are identi-
fied.   An examination of programmes and improved technologies already instituted reveals some of the causes of their success or
failure, from which it is possible to draw some conclusions about
the kinds of considerations that create a successful rural technology programme.

The problem

The population of Ghana is predominantly rural (75 per cent)
and extremely culturally and ethnically diverse.   The rural majority
lacks basic infrastructure in many critical areas, including transportation, electrification, water supply, health, education and
agriculture.   These shortages are so acute that life expectancy in
rural areas is 34 and 29 per cent lower than it is in urban areas,
for men and women respectively.   In addition, Ghana suffers from a
shortage of foreign exchange, a high inflation rate and has a population growth rate of 3.2 per cent.

Agriculture is the primary economic activity for most of the
Ghanaian people, and in the rural areas non-farm economic opportunities are extremely limited.   Women are the backbone of the
agricultural system in the south, where they grow maize, plantains,
cocoyams, cassava, vegetables and some cocoa as a cash crop.   Only
in the less fertile northern region is women's participation in
agriculture limited, partly because of the long hours they have to
work for water and firewood in this arid region.

These women's farms tend to be small-scale operations, which
produce at a very low rate of productivity.   Several factors contribute to this low productivity.   (1) They are too small to be
efficient.   (2) The women use rudimentary tools.   (3) Land tenure
systems tend to discriminate against women, allotting them small or

infertile plots.   (4) Technical assistance is not available to
women.   (5) The distance between the women's homes and farms means
they often have to walk between six and 12 miles roundtrip.   (6)
Women have to perform a range of onerous household duties in addition
to farming, which sap time and energy.   (7) Men traditionally clear
the land from the forest and in their absence (more frequent as a
result of migration), women must pay hired workers to do it.   Their
limited income usually causes a decrease in the amount they are able
to have cleared.   (8) Credit is not generally available to women.
The productivity level has dropped so low because of causes like
these that, although Ghana is an agricultural nation, she has been
forced to import foodstuffs for many years.   The agricultural
development projects thus far undertaken by the Government have been
based on complex and expensive, capital-intensive, imported technologies.   They have done little to address the problems faced by
the majority of people, particularly the women, as they have been
introduced on a very limited scale and utilise mainly male labour.
In addition, their huge expense has compounded the problem of foreign
exchange and inflation.

Since farming is the primary activity of most rural women, the
development of simple but improved agricultural technologies, that
they could use, would be the single greatest contribution to the
improvement of their living standard.   There are, however, several
other areas in which improved technology would go a long way.   Food
processing takes up a great deal of time and energy, as the techniques used are very slow, labour-intensive, inefficient and often
unhygienic.   Preservation of fish by smoking or drying, often a co-
operative venture between men, who catch the fish, and women who
preserve it, tends to be particularly unhygienic and inefficient.
Fish smoked by the traditional method loses much of its nutritive
value and leaves a high moisture content, thus resulting in wastage
through spoilage.   Gari (a common food) making is a highly labour-
intensive process, which requires the grating, pressing and cooking
of cassava.   Kokonte (cassava flour) production requires pounding
with a mortar and pestle, and a drying process that is also inefficient and unsanitary.   Cooking oil is obtained through pounding
and boiling various substances.   These are only a few examples of
the kinds of chores involved in food processing.

Unpaid household chores are another major burden on women that
improved technology could lighten considerably.   The search for

water can be long and the distance it is carried very far.   It is
often contaminated and many rural people suffer from diseases related
to the impure water supplies.   Firewood and other household fuels
must be gathered from far-flung areas in order for the women to even
begin some of their other duties, such as cooking.

Finally, non-agricultural, income-generating activities are
practised in different localities, which place more demands on the
women's time and energy.   Some of these are salt mining, soap
making, pottery and charcoal making.

Taking all these activities into account, the study finds that
women have very little time for rest or for participation in
political and other social activities as well as training programmes
mounted in the villages.   The effect on the women of these numerous
backbreaking chores is natural tiredness and constant complaint of
"chronic ailments, such as backache, headache, aching limbs, chest
pains and the like, and as the well-being of themselves and their
families depends so much on their maintaining their strength, life
indeed seems hard when they are feeling under the weather".
(Hardiman, 1974).

The success and failure of rural technical programmes

Some new technologies of an uncomplicated and inexpensive type
have been introduced on a limited scale to simplify these tasks.
Several varieties of smoking ovens have been developed to improve
fuel and work efficiency and the quality of the finished product.
Of these, the most widely accepted were the simplest and least
expensive, which varied little from the traditional mud ovens.
Raised drying racks to improve the hygiene, efficiency and quality
of sun-drying were easily introduced and accepted in a few areas.
Cassava graters and pressing machines as well as larger roasting
pans increased the output and efficiency of gari production in one
village.   A kiln to process the waste material used in soap making
greatly facilitated that process where it was introduced.

Other technologies, however, did not have such a high level of
success.   Hybrid maize seeds, designed for high productivity, were
rejected by the women because the maize tasted different, was more
difficult to process into the traditional dishes, was less resist-
ant to drought and insects and required heavy inputs of chemical
fertilisers.   New broadlooms were not used because weaving is

considered to be a man's job. The women believed that using the looms would render them infertile. The same was true of bullock ploughs. Traditional beliefs hold that if a woman touches cattle, she will become sterile.

Constraints and aids to successful adoption of new technologies

As we have seen from the successes and failures described above, the acceptance and success of the new technologies depends, not only on low cost and high return, but on simplicity and similarities with traditional practices. Those technologies that had the greatest success were those that were appropriate to the individuals (women) who used them, affordable by the women, and did not require a change in traditional beliefs, taboos, structures, procedures or values. Where the women themselves had participated in the earliest stages of the identification and design of the improved technologies shaping them according to the above criteria, they were usually accepted more quickly and easily.

Technologies introduced as part of a packet also tended to be more successful than those that were introduced individually. Packets included both supporting services, such as child care and credit, and a whole range of related technologies. Institutional child care is essential to ensure that new programmes, which require the mother to work away from home, do not put the burden of child care on the eldest daughters and thereby forcing them to forgo school. Credit, where available alongside of new technologies, makes them infinitely more affordable and, thus, available. The importance of taking the whole production process into consideration in packet design, including the socio-economic relationships it depends on, is clear in the example of gari-making. The women could produce so much more gari with the new tools, that a bottle-neck appeared in the cultivation of cassava. A men's cassava growing association was formed to step up cassava production.

Another constraint on the success of new technologies is in the area of dissemination. There are, however, many institutions, both new and old which could play an important role in this step. Small rural technology centres have the potential to spread improvements through the countryside and reach the rural people, who would be put off by urban or academic technology development institutes. Traditional organisations, of which there are many, have a major but underutilised potential to hasten the knowledge and acceptance of new processes.   Group leaders, or those who are traditionally the keepers of technical expertise, such as the village blacksmiths and carpenters, could also provide a valuable entry point for the dissemination and adoption of new tools and techniques.   A mass media campaign that utilised the radio and mobile cinema vans could include such traditional elements as "high life songs", which would, literally, sing the praises of new technologies.   Finally, new organisations, specifically village project committees, could have a major influence on the local level.   In order for any effective spread of improved technologies to take place, a number of these institutions will probably have to be activated.

The first step any dissemination or education programme will have to undertake is the consciousness-raising of the rural women. They must learn that the lifestyle they lead is unnecessarily arduous, and that programmes and institutions exist to help relieve them of some of the burden of their daily lives.

Conclusion

The range of factors that must be taken into account in identifying and assessing the appropriateness and potential of a new technology is wide.   It ranges from cultural and religious practices through scientific and economic realities.   Care must be taken in the examination and identification of women's work, the kinds of activities they perform and the techniques they use.   The organisation of production in the village as a whole, the division of labour between the sexes, classes and ages, can contribute to the success of a project if the project deals comprehensively with it.   However, it can limit the productivity, accessibility or practicality of individual technologies if not properly explored and dealt with.   Traditional religious beliefs and institutions have got to be examined, as they have tremendous potential to either help or hinder the acceptance and dissemination of new processes. It would also be of help to know what knowledge has already been disseminated, what projects have succeeded, and why, and how well the existing development agencies are functioning before a new project or technology is launched in an area.   Research into these areas is clearly of great value to Ghana and other African nations which share political, cultural, geographical and economic characteristics.   Given the expense and time required for such research, there appears to be a large role for international African organisations and co-operation between states in a research capacity.

BIBLIOGRAPHY

Addo, N.O.: Migration and Economic Change in Ghana, Vol. 1: Social and Demographic Characteristics of the Cocoa Farming Population of the Brong Ahafo Region (Legon, Demographic Unit, 1971).

Addo, N.O.: "Employment and labour supply on Ghana's cocoa farms, the pre- and post-Aliens Compliance Order", in Economic Bulletin of Ghana, Vol. 2, No. 2 (1972).

Adinku, V.: "Salt mining by women in the Keta area" (Legon, Department of Sociology, 1980).

Adomako-Sarfo, J.: "Migrant Asante cocoa farmers and their families", C. Oppong (ed.), in Legon Family Research Papers No. 1 (Institute of African Studies, Legon, 1974).

Afful, E.M.: "Investing in the food industries" in Proceedings of the First Seminar on Food Science and Technology in Ghana (1968).

Agarwal, B.C.: "Technological change and rural women in Third World agriculture: Some analytical issues and an empirical analysis" (University of Sussex Institute of Development Studies, 1980).

Ahmad, Z.: "The plight of rural women: Alternatives for action", in International Labour Review, Vol. 119, No. 4 (1980).

Ahmed, I.: Technological Change and the Condition of Rural Women, A Preliminary Assessment (WEP 2-22/WP 39, ILO, Geneva, 1978).

Akoso-Amaa, K.: Ghana/IDRC Rural Fishery Research and Development Project Research Report, No. 5 (Accra, Food Research Institute, 1976).

Ampratwum, D.B.: "Promotion of technology for improvement of rural life in Ghana", paper presented for trainers and planners on village technology for the rural family (Freetown, Sierra Leone, 1979).

Aryee, A.F.: "The migration factor in rural development strategy - The case of Ghana", paper presented at seminar on The Population Factor and Rural Development Strategy (Monrovia, 1980).

Asare, J.: "Making life easier for Africa's rural women", in Village Technology (UNICEF News, 1976).

Baron, C.G. (ed.): Technology, Employment and Basic Needs in Food Processing in Developing Countries (Oxford, Pergamon Press, 1980).

Beecham, A.: "The programme and operations of the Home Extension Unit Department of Agriculture, Ghana, in the field of appropriate technology", paper presented at a workshop for trainers and planners on village technology for the rural family (Freetown, Sierra Leone, 1979).

Bequele, A.: Poverty, Inequality and Stagnation: The Ghanaian Experience (WEP 10-6/WP 33, ILO, Geneva, 1980).

Birmingham, W., Neustadt, I., Omaboe, E.M. (ed.): A Study of Contemporary Ghana, Vols. 1 and 2 (London, Allen and Unwin, 1966).

Bogaards, J.N.: "Report on an inquiry into the farms of some Kusasi farmers", mimeo. (Deventer, Netherlands, Dec. 1969).

Boserup, E.: Women's Role in Economic Development (London, George Allen and Unwin, 1970).

Brokensha, D.: Social Change in Larteh (Oxford, Clarendon Press).

Brown, C.K.: "Strategies of rural development in Ghana", in Universitas (Legon, University of Ghana, 1974).

Bukn, J.: The Village Woman in Ghana (Uppsala, Scandinavian Institute of African Studies, 1979).

Campbell-Platt, G.: "The development of appropriate food technologies in Ghana: An overview", paper presented at Seminar on Ghanaian Women and Development (Accra, 1978).

Carr, M.: Economically Appropriate Technologies for Developing Countries: An Annotated Bibliography (London, Intermediate Technology Publications, 1976).

Carr, M.: "Preface", to S. Holtermann's Intermediate Technology in Ghana: The Experience of Kumasi, University's Technology Consultancy Centre (London, Intermediate Technology Publications Ltd., 1979).

Carr, M.: Technology and Rural Women in Africa (ILO, Geneva, 1980).

Central Bureau of Statistics, Population Census of Ghana, all volumes (Accra, Government printer, 1960).

--- Population Census of Ghana (Accra, Government printer, 1970).

Cole, J.: "National Council on Women and Development: Policies and actions" (Accra, NCWD, 1980).

Dadson, J.A.: "Farm size and the modernisation of agriculture in Ghana" in Ofori, I. (ed.), Factors of Agricultural Growth in West Africa (Legon, Institute of Statistics, Social and Economic Research, 1973).

Dalton, G.E. and Parker, R.N.: Agriculture in South-East Ghana, Vol. II (University of Reading, Department of Agricultural Economics and Management, 1978).

Date-Bah, E., Brown, C. and Gyeke, L.: Ghanaian Women and Co-operatives (Accra, Ghana National Council on Women and Development, 1978).

Date-Bah, E.: "Rural development and the status of women", paper presented at a seminar on The Role of Population Factor in the Rural Development Strategy (Monrovia, 1980).

Date-Bah, E.: "The changing work roles of Ghanaian women" (Accra, NCWD forthcoming, 1980).

Date-Bah, E. and Stevens, Y.: "Rural women in Africa and tech-
    nological change: Some issues" in Labour and Society, Vol. 6,
    No. 2 (Geneva, International Institute for Labour Studies,
    1981).

de Wilde, T.: "Some social criteria for appropriate technology"
    in Congdon, R.J.: Introduction to Appropriate Technologies
    (Rodale Press, 1977).

Dutta-Roy, D.K. and Mabey, S.J.: Household Budget Survey in Ghana
    (ISSER, Legon, 1968).

Ewusi, K.: "Women in occupations in Ghana", paper presented at a
    seminar on Ghanaian women and development (Accra, NCWD, 1978).

Fortes, M.: "Time and social structure: An Ashanti case study", in
    Fortes, M. (ed.), Social Structure (New York, Russell and
    Russell, 1949).

Foster, G.M.: Traditional Cultures and the Impact of Technological
    Change (New York, Harper Brothers, 1962).

Gaisie, S.K.: "Demographic trends in Ghana and world population
    plan of action" (Legon, 1980).

German Foundation for Developing Countries: Development and
    Dissemination of Appropriate Technologies in Rural Areas
    (Report on an international workshop held in Kumasi from
    17 to 18 July 1972).

Ghana National Council on Women and Development: The First Women's
    Co-operative Gari Factory (Accra, 1980).

Goody, J.: "Rice burning in Northern Ghana", in The Journal of
    Development Studies (1979).

Hagan, G.P.: "Divorce, polygamy and family welfare", in Ghana
    Journal of Sociology, Vol. 10, No. 1, 1976.

Hardiman, M.: "A preliminary study of the role of women in some
    Akan rural communities", in C. Oppong (ed.), Legon Family
    Research Papers (University of Ghana, Institute of African
    Studies, 1974).

Hevi-Yiboe, L.A.P.: Smoke in Rural Ghanaian Kitchens (Accra,
    Arakan Press, 1979).

Hill, P.: Migrant Cocoa Farmers of Southern Ghana (Cambridge
    University Press, 1963).

Holtermann, S.: Intermediate Technology in Ghana: The Experience
    of the Technology Consultancy Centre (London, Intermediate
    Technology Group, 1979).

ILO: "Tarkwa women's income generating activities: Draft report
    of evaluation mission" (Geneva, 1980).

ILO: Rural Technology Centres (Technology and Employment Branch,
    Geneva, 1980).

Jedlicka, A.D.: Organisation for Rural Development (New York,
    Praeger, 1977).

Kagan, B.: Fish Processing in Ghana: Possibilities of Improving Traditional Processing (Accra, Food Research and Development Unit, FAO, 1970).

Killick, A. and Szereszewski, R.: "The economy of Ghana", in Robson, P. and Lury, D.A. (ed.), The Economics of Africa, (London, George Allen and Unwin, 1969).

Killick, A.: Development Economics in Action: A Study of Economic Policies in Ghana (London, Heinemann, 1978).

Klingshirn, A.: "The changing position of women in Ghana", Doctoral dissertation (University of Marburg/Lahn, 1971).

Klingshirn, A.: "Investment of women in co-operatives in Zaire and Ghana" (UNFPA/FAO Study, 1978).

Konadu, O.: "A study of a rural industry: The Adinkra industry in the Kwabre district of Ashanti", M.A. thesis (Department of Sociology, University of Ghana, Legon, 1980).

Lawson, R. and Kwei, E.: African Entrepreneurship and Economic Growth: A Case Study of the Fishing Industry of Ghana (Accra, Ghana Universities Press, 1974).

Mclean, K.: Fufu Preparation Machinery (Accra, FAO Food Research and Development Unit, 1968).

Mickelwait, D., Fiegelman, M. and Sweet, C.: Women in Rural Development (Colorado, Westview Press, 1976).

North, J., March, J., Mickelwait, D. and Street, C.: Women in National Development in Ghana (Accra, USAID, 1975).

Nukunya, G.K. and Boateng, E.O.: "An evaluation/study of water utilisation behaviour and its related socio-economic impact" (Institute of Statistical Social and Economic Research, University of Ghana, 1979).

Okali, C. and Mabey, S.: "Women in agriculture in southern Ghana", in Manpower and Unemployment Research in Africa, Vol. 8 (No. 2) (McGill University, 1975).

Ollennu, N.A.: "Aspects of land tenure", in Birmingham, W., Meustadt, I. and Omaboe, E.N. (ed.), A Study of Contemporary Ghana (London, Allen and Unwin, 1967).

Oluwasanmi, H.A.: "West African agricultural development in the 60s", in Ofori, I. (ed.), Factors of Agricultural Growth in West Africa (Legon, Institute of Statistical, Social and Economic Research, 1973).

Opare, K.D.: "The impact of agricultural extension services on rural development", paper prepared for Population Dynamics Programme Seminar on Population and Development (New Year School, Legon, 1979-80).

Oppong, C.: Marriage among a Matrilineal Elite (Cambridge University Press, 1974).

Oppong, C.: Seven Roles and Status of Women (ILO, Geneva, 1980).

Oppong, C.: "Changing roles of women in urban households: Action-
    oriented research on economic opportunities for women and
    demographic change" (ILO, Geneva, 1980).

Oppong, C., Okali, C. and Houghton, E.: "Women power: Retrograde
    steps in Ghana", in African Studies Review, Vol. XVIII, No. 3
    (Brandeis University, 1975).

Pala, A.O., Reynolds, J.E., Wallis, M.A. and Browne, D.L.: The
    Women's Group Programme in the SRDP, IDS Occasional Paper
    No. 13 (University of Nairobi, 1975).

Palmer, I.: "Rural women and the basic needs approach to develop-
    ment", in International Labour Review, Vol. XV, No. 3 (Geneva,
    ILO, 1977).

Parker, R.N.: "Catchment systems for rural water supplies", in
    Dalton, G.E. and Parker, R.N. (ed.), Agriculture in South East
    Ghana (Reading University, 1978).

Posnansky, M.: "How Ghana's crisis affects a village", in West
    Africa (1 December 1980).

Quraishy, B.B.: "Land tenure and economic development in Ghana",
    in Présence Africaine, No. 77, 1st quarterly (1971).

Sarpong, P.: Ghana in Retrospect: Some Aspects of Ghanaian
    Culture (Accra, Ghana Publishing Corporation, 1974).

The Legon Society on National Affairs: The Legon Observer,
    19 September to 2 October (Accra, Liberty Press, 1980).

The Republic of Ghana: Development Plan, 1950 to 1960 (Accra,
    Government Printer, 1951).

--- The Second Development Plan: 1959 to 1964 (Accra, Government
    Printer, 1959).

--- The Seven-Year Development Plan, 1963/64 to 1969/70 (Accra,
    Government Printer, 1963).

--- The Five-Year Development Plan: 1975/76 to 1979/80 (Accra,
    Government Printer, 1977).

Twumasi, P.A. et al: "A sociological study of rural water use",
    A project report for Ghana Water Supply and Environmental
    Health (Legon, 1977).

Vellenga, D.: "Differentiation among women farmers in two rural
    areas in Ghana", in Labour and Society (International Labour
    Institute, Geneva, 1977).

Vercruijsse, E.: "Fishmongers, big dealers and fishermen: Co-
    operation and conflict between the sexes in Ghanaian canoe
    fishing", in C. Oppong (ed.), Male and Female in West Africa
    (Allen and Unwin Ltd., forthcoming).

Wagenbur, H.T.M.: "Labour and development (an analysis of the time
    budget and of the production and productivity of lime farmers
    in southern Ghana)", Social Studies Project, Research Report
    Series No. 17 (University of Cape Coast, Ghana, 1972).

Woodman, G.: "The development of customary land law in Ghana",
    Ph.D. Thesis (Cambridge University, 1966).

Chapter 5

WOMEN'S ACCESS TO RESOURCES IN THE IVORY COAST:
WOMEN AND LAND IN ADIOUKROU DISTRICT*

by

Aminata Traoré

Introduction

Technological, economic and social change have everywhere
affected the kinds and quantity of resources available to rural
women.   The effects on land availability have been particularly
important, as land is the ultimate life-supporting resource.   This
paper explores the changes in the resources available to rural women
from the province of Adioukrou, the Ivory Coast, in a historical context.   Without this context, it is impossible to understand the
situation these women find themselves in and the import of the
activities they engage in.   The colonial experience and the process
of agro-industrialisation after independence, as this report describes,
effectively destroyed many of the socio-economic institutions of pre-
colonial Ivory Coast.   The women have turned to the production of a
traditional foodstuff for sale in a commercial market.   In this new
industry, however, the resources they have access to are restricted
by the ideology surrounding their traditional roles, the division
of labour and the lack of much needed infrastructure and technical
assistance directed towards women.

The traditional economy and the
division of labour

The land tenure system in pre-colonial Adioukrou was based on
the principle that no one should be denied access to land, the
resource that provided life itself.   Private ownership of land did
not exist - the local chief distributed the right to exploit land.
Under this system, men and women alike were guaranteed access to
land and other needed resources.   The extended family usually based
on matrilineal or bilineal ties was the most common production unit,
and men and women contributed equally to its subsistence.   The
importance of the concept of family units in the pre-colonial era is
particularly clear in the production of palm oil.

Palmeries were clan-owned and operated.   Everyone in the
family participated in the collection and extraction although there
was a division of labour between the men and women.   Palm oil pro-

---

* French language original.

duction was an important social event and the palmeries a social
centre.   Although men were exclusively responsible for marketing
the palm oil, they always returned a portion of the money earned to
the women, in recognition of their considerable contribution to the
production process.   In addition, the women got to keep the palm
kernels, from which they extracted another kind of oil used in household consumption.

The cultivation of other crops was also based on a division of
labour, although both sexes were extremely active.   Cassava, yams,
groundnuts and a number of other crops were cultivated for consumption, and cocoa and coffee were often raised as cash crops.   Men
were primarily responsible for clearing the land, felling and burning the trees.   After that, however, the jobs of planting, weeding,
harvesting and processing the crops were largely the women's.

Within the clan organisation, women were subordinate to men.
They were not expected to live alone or be independent.   However,
their important contribution to the economy of the clan was appre-
ciated.   The clan system provided a safety net for everyone, no
one, man, woman or child, was denied access to resources if he or
she had need.   Women as they reached old age were incorporated into
the formal family decision-making council.

Changes under colonial rule

The colonial era made some important changes in this socio-
economic organisation, some of which affected the women's position
dramatically.   Adioukrou, however, is unique among the provinces
in the respect that its high productive capacity in palm oil allowed
it to establish export and trade ties without major reorganisation
of its social and economic institutions.   Thus, the colonial period
did not have the same deep-seated effects it did in other provinces.

None the less, colonialism did push women toward the margin of
the production process in a few ways.   The single greatest change
the French made was the introduction of the concept of private
ownership of land.   The expansion of coffee and cocoa plantations
changed the whole concept of land from that which gives life to
that which provides income.   With this change in the value of land,
went the loss of the belief in the right of every individual to have
access to it.   Traditional rights of succession to land use were
undermined as a result.

The plantation system also brought with it the institution of wage labour. Plantations, however, hired only men, and where women did participate in plantation work, their husbands or fathers received their wages. Thus, the colonial period sharpened the division of labour between men, who received wages for their work, and women who generally remained in subsistence farming.

Even under the strain of the colonial system, the basic clan structure and division of labour remained effective. Palm oil production, the major group activity of the extended family, was not affected. It was with the imposition of the Government-sponsored palm oil refineries that these women became truly marginalised in the rural production process.

Independence and the palm oil project

In 1963, shortly after independence, the Government initiated a land reform programme in which they appropriated all the land not cultivated under the traditional land use system, and distributed it to whomever was willing to farm it, an idea they got from the French who tried the same thing. The goal of this programme was to increase and diversify the agricultural economy. Under this system, however, only 10 per cent of the land was cultivated, as the local people did not have the resources at their disposal to make cultivation profitable. The Government itself, then began to invest in major agricultural works, establishing large palm oil refineries under the direction of a government palm-oil development agency, SODEPALM. These refineries completely overturned the traditional socio-economic organisation of Adioukrou. A great deal of land was replanted with increased yield varieties of palm nut trees; the entire family organisation of the palmeries was done away with. New land divisions were created so that the palm nuts could be transported to the processing plants easily, and in the process, the land that was traditionally available to the women for subsistence was appropriated. These palmeries, however, did not provide either an alternate source of subsistence, income or employment to the women. They are capital-intensive, and much of the work that was formerly done by hand is done by the machines. The work that is left is done completely by men, with the exception of transporting the clusters to the factory, which is done by everyone. Men, however, receive the wages for all the work done by members of their families.

Under the new system, women receive a small compensation for the work that they do - from their husbands. This is usually a very small amount and tends to take the form of a "gift". The ideology behind this reward system is left over from the traditional clan structure and division of labour. Women are not viewed as wage earners. Their work is supposed to be done entirely within the context of the household. They maintain the household in exchange for the provision of certain necessities, shelter, clothing and food, which the man guarantees. Thus, their work in the palmeries is viewed as a contribution to the household, and not as labour that ought to be rewarded with a wage.

Along with the reorganisation of the production processes in the countryside, the Government undertook a sweeping legal reform. Women were granted equal rights before the law; most notably, women were given the right to be their own legal actors. However, there is still a large gap between theory and practice in regard to these laws and reforms. As seen in the example above, women are legally entitled to earn wages, but tradition prevails.

The production of attiéké as an alternative survival strategy

The persistence of need under the new system

Although the new palm oil factories are viewed as successful by the Government and economists, they have had seriously detrimental effects on the position of the women of Adioukrou. These women have increasing cash needs, for education, health care (both traditional and modern) and a range of other necessary goods and services.

The resources available to them have been severely curtailed by the reorganisation of palm oil production, and they must rely more and more on bought commodities. At the same time, their cash incomes have been almost eliminated. They continue to bear most of the burden for the maintenance of the household and the children on slimmer and slimmer resources. In order to augment their incomes, therefore, they have turned to the production and marketing of attiéké, a common food made from cassava (manioc).

The production and commercialisation of attiéké

Attiéké making is a long and laborious process. It takes three days to make one batch and the women are continuously producing it.   The cassava must be transported from the fields, washed, ground, pressed, dried and must undergo a number of other processes. Most of the processes are carried out by hand and are difficult and arduous.   Those that are done by machine, such as grinding, cost money and take a significant cut out of the final profits.

While undertaking the production of attiéké, the woman is not released from all her other duties toward the family.   She must still cook, wash, gather wood and water and take care of the children, all of which adds up to a long and exhausting work day.   It is not uncommon for women to work 14-16 hours just to accomplish the day's essential tasks.

The final profit from attiéké production is well below what the work deserves and what the market price should make it.   There are three major reasons for this.   The first lies in the traditional division of labour, which still persists in the area of subsistence farming.   Production for the market requires a much larger supply of cassava than the women previously cultivated.   They are unable to cultivate more themselves because they lack access to prepared land.   Although there is land available for them to use, it must be cleared, a job that is traditionally done by the men or by hired labour.   The women simply do not have the resources at their disposal to clear land for their own use in the cultivation of cassava. They, therefore, are dependent on men to sell them cassava.

Women are also dependent on a number of services in the production of attiéké, for which they must pay.   The most expensive of these are the grinding, which is done at a local mill to which women must carry the cassava, and transportation to the town for sale.

Finally, the women most often sell the attiéké to a local wholesaler, who reaps a considerable profit from the resale.   A breakdown of the costs of production and the return to the women gives some idea of the extent to which they are exploited.   Of the final retail price for one pannier of attiéké, which is between F9,000 and 10,000, the women receive between F1,000 and 2,000.   The cassave costs F3,000; the mill charges F500; transport takes an additional F1,000; there are miscellaneous costs of F500, and the wholesaler gets F3,000.

The role of improved technology
and co-operatives in attiéké
production

Several attempts have been made by the women themselves and by
various government and private institutions to improve the conditions under which attiéké is produced and marketed. Thus far,
however, none of them have proved successful. A local co-operative,
CODERDA, attempted in 1975 to rationalise the marketing methods
of the women. It collected the attiéké in the villages, paying
the women almost the full market value on the spot. It then transported it to the city, where it was sold directly to local institu-
ions, without any intermediaries. However, CODERDA quickly encountered difficulties and was forced to discontinue operation
after only a few weeks. Their major problems included the inability to store attiéké, which must be consumed within 24 hours,
therefore making it necessary to sell a great deal of attiéké
every day. They also had difficulty with the elderly people they
employed to load and unload the trucks. Finally, the task of re-
distributing the panniers to the women in the villages at the end
of the day, after the attiéké was sold, was a logistical nightmare.

Another project was recently instituted by the Government.
It, however, suffers from the same shortsightedness that the palm
oil programme does. Many acres were given over to the cultivation,
with mechanical farm machinery, of cassava. The cassava is then
harvested and brought to a factory for processing into attiéké.
Women and men are employed in the cultivation and transport of
cassava, but under many of the same inequalities found in the palm
oil refineries. Women do not participate in all tasks and their
husbands may receive their wages. The attiéké produced is different in form from that produced in the traditional manner, and most
of it is destined for export. This project is in danger of further
unbalancing the sexual division of labour and alienating women from
one more source of needed income. The full effects are still un-
known, however, as the project is only in the beginning stages.

The women themselves have been experimenting with the cultivation of other cash crops as a source of income. Many alternatives
have yet to be explored.

Finally, there are several simple and cheap technologies that
can be used within the home or village by the women. These technologies are now being investigated by the same institute that

began the attiéké mechanisation programme, in response to what they
perceive to be problems with that programme.

Conclusion

The state intervention in the economically important palmerie
project seems to have had detrimental effects upon the household
activities of women, their socio-economic situation and their
position vis-à-vis land.   The new land holding system penalises
women who do not control inputs and other productive factors.

The production of attiéké by the women of Adioukrou is clearly
an attempt by them to meet their needs in a situation that has
stripped them of many of the customary resources.   There are, however, many problems with the solution they have found.   These problems lie in both the areas of production and marketing, and they
stem from cultural and economic sources.   The women themselves
recognise the need to reverse the deterioration of their conditions
of life.   The experience of CODERDA and the other projects demonstrates that this is possible, but that formidable obstacles must
be attacked in the process.   To overcome all these obstacles,
successful change must go in several directions.   Planners, particularly technical experts, must be educated as to the special needs of
women, and the restrictions imposed on them.   They must learn that
women constitute an active part of the rural economy, and their
technical plans must encompass that part, while recognising that
agricultural policies cannot be based solely on the profit motive.

In the special case of the attiéké makers, there are a number
of specific changes that could immediately and directly improve
their position.   The reorganisation of attiéké marketing, along
the lines of the CODERDA programme, would, by eliminating the need
for middle men and the costs of transportation, increase the women's
share of profit in what is essentially their industry.   The women
themselves have shown an ability to organise effectively, as they
were active in the CODERDA programme from the beginning.   A co-
operative collection system, if it receives proper resources and
technical advice on the logistical aspects of marketing and co-
ordination, has tremendous potential.   Such a co-operative also
has the potential to improve the conditions under which attiéké is
made, reducing the cost and improving the quality.   Finally, with
improved quality, transportation and storage facilities, there is a
large export market to be explored.

BIBLIOGRAPHY

AFIRD-LAJP: Problèmes fonciers en Afrique Noire: Rapport introductif aux journées d'études du 22 au 23 septembre 1980 à Paris.

ESSOH, G.: La filière artisanale de l'attiéké de Dabou à Abidjan (Mémoire de DEA d'Economie rurale, Université de Montpellier, Oct. 1980).

KINDO, B.: Economie de plantation chez l'agni de l'Indénié (Université d'Abidjan, Institut de Géographie tropicale, juin 1973).

KOBY ASA, Th.: Système géographique et problématique des espaces ethnoculturels ivoiriens: exemple du pays adioukrou (Thèse de 3ème cycle de Bordeaux IV, Jan. 1980).

LEY, A.: Le régime domanial et foncier et le développement économique de la Côte d'Ivoire, Librairie Générale de Droit et de Jurisprudence. (Paris, R. Lichon et E. Durand Anzias, 1972).

Meillassoux, Cl.: Femmes, greniers et capitaux (Paris, François Maspero, 1975).

Ministère de l'agriculture: Plantations villageoises de palmiers à huile (SODEPALM).

Idem: Projet de développement de la culture du manioc dans la région des Baoulé (July 1977).

Sawadogo, A.: L'Agriculture en Côte d'Ivoire (Paris, Presses Universitaires de France, 1977).

Chapter 6

THE IMPACT OF TERRITORIAL ADMINISTRATION REFORM
ON THE SITUATION OF WOMEN IN SENEGAL*

by

Fama Hane Ba, Aminata Mbengue Ndiaye,
Marie-Angélique Savane and Awa Thiongane,
with the assistance of Marème Deme, Ciré Sow,
Marie Angélique Sarr, Faye Bèye Diack,
Oumou Khaïry Ly and Saliétou Toure

Introduction

In 1964, the Government of Senegal undertook a comprehensive
land and administrative reform.   The goals of the administrative
reform programme were to build adequate state structures in the
rural areas, that could absorb and organise the participation of all
people, and to readapt the urban state mechanisms of participation
and correct their management of state affairs.   Hand in hand with
the administrative reform went a land reform programme designed to
correct some of the inefficiencies and inequalities of the existing
land distribution.   Senegal's development programme now revolves
around the new administrative regions.   One of the fundamental
ideas upon which the reforms are based is the equal participation of
all members of society in development programmes and equal gains
from the results.

The region of Thies was the first to undergo reform, and now,
seven years after the initiation of the programmes, this report
attempts to evaluate how well the administrative reform has met its
goal of equal participation in administrative and development policy
for rural women in Thies.   Five rural communities in three departments are included in this study.   In each of these rural communities several villages were studied over a period of 12 months, in
order to take account of the great diversity of culture and background of the peoples of the area.   The rural communities included
are Jander, Fandene and Ndiender Guedj in the district of Pout (the
most heavily industrialised province under the national industrial
development plan), in the département of Thies;   Nguekokh, in the
province of the same name in the département of Mbour;   and Noto
Gouye Diama, in the province of Pambal in the département of
Tivaoune.

---

* French language original.

Traditional and colonial land tenure and administration

The population of Thies is extremely diverse in its tribal and religious background. Many of the traditional laws concerning women and their rights to land use vary from region to region and from village to village. However, there are a few universal characteristics. Land tenure in pre-colonial Senegal was based on the communal or family ownership of land. Land itself was un- alienable, and only its use was passed on from person to person or household to household. The village head or family chief was res- ponsible for overseeing the distribution of land. Usually land use rights were passed on from father to son. Rules concerning the women's rights to own or inherit land varied from region to region, but, in general, women did not have the right to do so. It was very rare for a woman to own or control land. In some places, women were prohibited from owning any substantial property, and their only possessions were those things necessary to the maintenance of their household.

Under this system, however, women had the right to work the land allotted to their husbands or fathers.

Over a period of time, religious and political pressures caused a considerable amount of migration in the area. The result of this was the existence of a class of landless people, even before the colonial era.

Under the French, the monetisation of the economy, especially the commercialisation of land, made it even more difficult for women to obtain land, as they did not have access to capital with which to buy it, and access to land was more strictly controlled.

The French colonial administration instituted a land reform programme of its own. However, they were remarkably unsuccessful in enforcing it. Despite their efforts, the traditional land tenure system continued, in a modified form. At the time of independence, only 1 per cent of the land was properly registered with the colonial authorities.

Land and administrative reform

In 1964, the independent Government instituted a land reform system in order to take account of and make productive all the land that was unregistered and to ensure a more equal distribution.

Under this reform programme, the Government appropriated all the
land that was not public property or already privately registered.
The organs of the rural communities (administrative divisions)
were to allot the land to those who could demonstrate that they
would cultivate it.   This law was the beginning of the rural communities, and the first division of Senegal along these administrative lines.

In 1972, the concept of the rural community was modified to
what it exists as today.   The 1972 legislation set up guidelines
by which the administration of the rural communities was to take
place.   Each rural community has a Council and a Council President.
Two-thirds of the Council members are elected by popular suffrage,
and the remaining third is elected by the general assembly of the
land co-operatives.   The Rural Council is responsible for advice
and discussion in many areas, but cannot legislate without the con-
sent of the central Government.   It's sphere of activity includes
planning and zoning matters, licenses for the use of resources,
regulation of gifts and bequests, the budget for the Rural Council,
projects for rural development, regulation of acquisitions,
management of public places, protection of land and resources
against poachers, fire fighting and resource and water control.
The President, as a representative of the subprefect, has authority
over the traditional village heads, who are still active on the
village level.   All members of the Rural Council are unpaid.

Problems with the implementation of
the reform programme

The success of the reform programmes has varied greatly from
place to place.   In some areas, the problems have been more un-
expected or difficult than in others, but some of the more common
and difficult problems are described below.

The rural councils are often ineffective political bodies.
They have little internal organisation and often come to be dominated
by two opposing groups.   In such a situation, a stalemate results,
and the Rural Council is unable to legislate on anything.

Among the councillors themselves, there is little understanding
of the nature of their post.   Although they are elected to represent the entire rural community, they consider themselves the representatives of their own villages.   They, therefore, approach problems with the interest of their village in mind, which makes legisla-

tion in the general interest of the region as a whole impossible.
It also means that the villages which have no representative in the
Rural Council do not get represented.

Legislation that is intended to protect the integrity of the
rural councils has in some cases backfired and proven to be an
obstacle to the effective functioning of those bodies.   The
President of the Rural Council is not allowed to live in the central
town, for fear that that town would monopolise that post.   However,
the effect of this is to force the President to travel frequently
from his home village, and in Thies rural transportation is poor or
completely non-existent.   Thus the time spent in travelling or trying to travel prohibits the Council President from fulfilling his
duties completely.

In addition, the Council members are not paid for their services.
This is a device meant to exclude all those seeking office for
material gain.   However, it makes the position of councillor a
difficult one to hold, especially for those who do not come from
larger villages, the scattered peasants who have fewer resources
to command.   When we consider that the village head retains a
portion of the taxes collected, it is clear that the new system
discriminates against the most rural segments of the population.

Among the entire rural population, including the Rural Council
itself, there is a lack of understanding of the idea of the reform
and the division of authority between the village heads and the
Rural Council.   This problem is aggravated by the fact that all the
Government texts on the reform are in French, in which most of the
rural population is illiterate.

The lack of understanding of the Rural Council's role stems, in
part, from the failure of the land reform, which was meant to take
place simultaneously.   People have begun to see the Rural Council
as a means to further their own interests with regard to the land
reform.   Thus far, the presidents of the rural councils of the five
rural communities under study have not legislated once in the favour
of a landless family.   No land has been appropriated and redistributed according to the law.   In Jander, practically all the land
was already under cultivation by the time of the land reform.   A
group of politically active farmers ("les Lamanes"), foreseeing the
land reform and its particularities, had begun to cultivate almost
all the land in the area, largely by planting fruit trees on it just
before the vote in the National Assembly setting the land reform in

action.   The rest of the land they either sold to state agents or
claimed was of religious significance and should not be disturbed.
Thus, when it came time for redistribution, the President of the
Rural Council of Jander had no land available to redistribute.

The final problem the rural councils have had, affecting the
entire rural population, is the budget.   Because of their lack of
cohesion and a generally low-level of education, the rural councils
have been unable to draw up the budgets for the rural communities
themselves, and seven years after the administrative reform, the
office of the subprefect still does it for them.   When the rural
councils were first set up, the budget was to be in the hands of the
subprefect until the rural councils were sufficiently organised to
take over.   However, that time has never arrived.

Given all these problems, the most visible effects of the rural
councils is the presence of certain types of infrastructure.   The
new schools and community centres are perceived by the population as
the work of the rural councils, and to many of the rural people, the
provision of such services is seen as the only function of the
Council, especially in Jander, where the Council is responsible for
the construction of 17 classrooms and a system of health care.
Neither one of these creations has been problem free, but they are,
thus far, the most visible effects of the existence of the Rural
Council.

The administrative reforms and rural women

One of the primary goals of the reformers was the increased
participation of all sectors and classes of the population in the
development and administration of the rural communities.   In many
cases, including that of women, this meant the activation of previously politically excluded groups.

However, the concern with the condition of rural women is not
directly approached in the reform texts.   Rather, reforms concerning
women are made within the context of the traditional, patriarchal
family system.   As a result, the reforms have reached women even
less than they have reached the rest of the population.   There are
very few women on the rural councils (out of 500 councillors in the
communities of Nguekokh, Noto Gouye Diama, Fandene and Ndiender
Guedj, there are four women), and by and large, women are completely
ignorant of the law and the reforms.   They don't know their repre-

sentative, who is almost always male, and they have never seen him. He does not reach or inform them.

Although women are a very large majority of registered voters, they always concede to men in the actual voting. If women were to vote together and in autonomy, there could be as many as two women to every man on the Rural Council.

The economic effects of the reform have not been much better than the political ones for the women of Thies. Although their original position with regard to access to resources and means of production varied tremendously according to the diverse traditions of the area, most of them were considerably deprived. In many areas, women were prohibited from controlling or inheriting land, the single most important resource. With the growth of the migrant population, women's position deteriorated even more, for women of these families were no longer even assured access to land.

Under the reform, women are still not generally granted access to land. Where land reform has actually taken place, the land has been given neither to the poorest families nor to women. Men are the only recipients of redistributed land.

Traditionally women were largely involved in agricultural activities. Most were small-scale farmers, growing vegetables in the subsistence sector. Some were engaged in petty trade of dairy products. For them, the greatest problem has always been the lack of transportation to and from their markets.

With the spread of cash cropping, women became more and more responsible for the subsistence sector. At the same time, however, they were forced to help their husbands with the commercial crops, and had less and less time for their own activities.

The introduction of some new technologies, such as the plough and seeders, have saved a considerable amount of time in some cases. But the new technologies are almost universally introduced in traditionally male sectors, and women only benefit when they are released from helping their husbands. Where they have been released from some work, women have been able to invest that time in commercial vegetable production. As yet, however, there are only traditional hand tools and techniques available to these women, and water availability is a continual problem. Combined with the transportation problem, these shortages make commercial vegetable farming not very profitable, but the activity does provide some cash income, without which they would be much worse off.

Some other forms of income-generating employment have been provided for women, such as work in the palmeries.   But again, this is
not very profitable, and women are expected to contribute their income to the survival of the household, for they cannot always expect
the contribution of the male members.

Perhaps one of the most effective reforms has been the organisation of women into production groups.   These groups are designed to
better the conditions of life and improve child care for the rural
women.   At times, these groups have allowed women to organise communal mills to cut down on the time involved in housework, and they
have helped women receive funds for their own projects.

The production groups, however, have many of their own problems.
Among them are the shortage of storage space for goods especially
perishables, to be marketed, marketing skills and transportation.
They also tend to be organised around the training of traditional
women's activities, such as handicrafts which do not allow women to
break out of their traditional and limited roles.   Again, in these
areas, women's profits are small, because of the marketing and production constraints.

Despite all of these problems, the women's groups have managed
to stick together.   Women feel committed to them, and try hard to
make them work.   Several of them have managed to make a considerable
profit out of their enterprises.

At the root of many of the failures of the reforms on the
political and economic positions of women is its failure to significantly change the social and familial position of women.   The traditional family structures are by and large patriarchal; women are
subservient to men in every sphere.   Marriages are polygamous among
several groups, but in these groups women see polygamy as a way to
cut down on the household work by sharing it with several other women.
In all the groups women's primary role and responsibility is that of
wife and mother.

Reform of the women's place in the family has barely begun.
There is a new family code with clauses that are designed to protect
women.   However, women are generally ignorant of the code, and where
they are aware of it they ignore it, for to try to enforce it and
attempt a divorce, for example, would be a very socially unwise move.
As a last resort, the civil code can be and is used as protection
against forced marriages.

Conclusion

Women, contrary to the widespread idea that they do not participate in the economic development process, do participate at two
levels:

(i)   directly in the production activities and

(ii) indirectly in reproducing the labour force and in assuring
      its maintenance.

Unfortunately, despite women's active participation, there is
still room for more involvement, particularly at the political level.
Women have to be aware of their situation and make sure that their
rights are recognised.   Women, after the reform, still do not have
access to the means of production.   The production groups, which
are a good starting point to make women more independent, are
nevertheless not integrated within a more coherent overall policy
nor do they have access to resources which would be instrumental
for their development.

If the participation of women is to be achieved within the
context of the reforms, several steps must be taken.   The presence
of women on the rural councils has great potential for the improvement of their position.   However, the effectiveness of the rural
councils must first be improved, perhaps through better information
provision, both to the councillors themselves and to the population
as a whole.   This might also be achieved, and would, no doubt, be
most effectively achieved, without the aid of legislation providing
for the mandatory presence of women on the councils, but through the
organisation of the female voting population.

The creation of women's foyers and meeting places could also
contribute to the emancipation of women.   There must, however, be
a concerted attempt for them to be so, and they must be perceived
by the reformers as centres of emancipation.   The community buildings, now only used for the meetings of the rural councils and
receiving foreigners, could also be used as a meeting place for
local groups, including women's groups, while special foyers are
being built.   These centres must go beyond the current activities
of the women's production groups, for as effective as the groups
are, they do not address the fundamental questions of access to
resources and the effective organisation and participation of women
in the politics and development of the rural areas.

BIBLIOGRAPHY

Bouffil, F.:   Reflexions sur le paysanat sénégalais et son
    amélioration possible (unpublished).

Conseil économique et social: Etude complémentaire sur le rôle et
    la place de la femme sénégalaise dans le développement
    (Dakar, 1975).

Copans, J., Couty, Ph., Roch, J., Rocheteau, G.: Maintenance
    sociale et changement économique au Sénégal: doctrine du
    travail chez les Mourides (Paris, ORSTOM, 1973).

Lericollais, A.: Sob Etudes géographique d'un terroir Serer
    (Paris, Mouton, 1972).

N'diaye, A.: La province de Jander de 1861 à 1885, Mémoire de
    Maîtrise (Université de Dakar, Faculté de Lettres et Sciences
    humaines, 1976).

Pélissier: Les paysans du Sénégal (Saint-Yriex, Imprimerie Fabrégue,
    1966).

Vidal, C.: Dossier préliminaire: projet de vulgarisation en
    milieu féminin rural dans les opérations de développement
    (Dakar, SODEVA, July 1972).

RURAL DEVELOPMENT PLANNING AND THE SEXUAL
DIVISION OF LABOUR: A CASE STUDY OF A
MOSLEM HAUSA VILLAGE IN NORTHERN NIGERIA

by

Richard Longhurst

Introduction

Development in many low-income countries appears not to have
led to improvements in the incomes of many groups in rural areas.
A better understanding of the division of labour by·sex, age or
income group will show how resources are distributed between and
within families, and, if it can be translated into policy, should
lead to a more equitable distribution towards impoverished groups.
Differences between groups in ownership of resources such as land,
labour, grain and other assets, in returns to occupations and in
access to credit, institutions and power holding will determine the
rates at which groups acquire economic power. This study focuses
on the sexual division of labour, i.e. differences in work done by
men and women, their returns to work and their access to productive
resources. It also involves examining the sets of obligations
between men and women, especially in the household and in marriage
all within the social and economic structure of the community in
which they live.

To date, rural and agricultural development in developing
countries has tended to serve a relatively homogeneous clientele,
usually the male farmer growing large areas of cash crops. The
family has always been considered as the basic economic unit and
most projects and policies have been designed on this basis.

Now the need is to reach large numbers of rural people by
projects and policies that should have several goals other than
only increases in physical production, such as employment creation
and the provision of health, nutrition and social service facilities
(popularly known as "basic needs"). Such an approach has to
recognise particular groups as its target, rather than being a
strategy that introduces resources believed to bring about production increases somewhere and sometime among some groups of the
population. Therefore such a strategy has to recognise the considerable differences in culture and socio-economic status that can
exist within the project area; the diversity in potential

beneficiaries in resource holdings and therefore in ability to
adopt, and respond to, economic incentives implies similar diversity
in planning and project design.   These suggest that it is necessary
to disaggregate the family as the basic decision-making unit and
examine the factors affecting the sexual division of labour as an
integral part of a successful rural development policy which has a
diverse population as its target group.

The case study area

This research was conducted in a village which shall be called
Wurinkada in Kaduna State in the north of Nigeria.   The village was
50 miles west of Kano, the second largest city in Nigeria, and 20
miles from the town of Malumfashi.   It was situated on a tarmac
road at a crossroads with an unpaved road.   It was the headquarters
of a village area; the village head was resident here and this
village and five hamlets were under his control.   It is fairly
unusual in the quantity and quality of its contact with the outside
world.

A.   Social structure

This village, Wurinkada, is a completely Moslem village.
Women are considered to be minors until they marry, and after
marriage, the division of labour is according to Moslem law.   Men
are responsible for the provision of food, shelter, clothing and
water, and women are expected to provide all the household labour,
including food preparation, child care and washing, as well as
bearing children.   This division of labour is more or less loosely
adhered to by most of the families in the village although men in
particular are likely to be lax in the fulfilment of their duties.
Marriages are also virilocal and polygamous.   The practice of
seclusion of women has been spreading in recent years.

Within the village, there is a complex family and occupational
class system.   Men are the individuals who take part in this class
system, and a family's position in the hierarchy depends only on the
position and activities of the man.

There is a great difference between men's and women's access
to land.   Daughters are legally entitled to inherit land from their
fathers, but usually receive only half of what their brothers
inherit, and their portion may be entirely substituted by cash

payments from brothers. Women do not generally inherit land from their husbands. The relation of women to land is very complicated: there are different forms of landholding by women. Customs vary considerably; and full information is difficult to obtain.

Credit is also not generally available to women. They may, however, borrow from their husbands. No formal credit is normally available to them. The capital they can sometimes rely on is that which they have brought with them on their marriage. Additional sources of credit for women are those generated by them by means of savings societies (adashi).

Since divorce in Wurinkada is easy and common, women hold a very shaky position in the village. If they are divorced, the only permanent option open to them is remarriage. Their natal families will support them for a while until they find a new husband. There is no room in the village for a single woman.

Perhaps the most unusual aspect of the social organisation in Wurinkada is the overwhelming cash orientation of the economy. Women may borrow from their husbands, and frequently there are cash transactions between husband and wife where there is an exchange of goods or labour between them. This is related to the desire of women for financial independence in the polygamous society where it is relatively easy for the husband to get a divorce.

The sexual division of labour is very clear-cut in Wurinkada. Separation takes place according to occupation, but particularly by physical location. Women are not supposed to interact with men, or even leave their household compound during the day, in some cases. Where women work for wages, whether in separate tasks or the same as men, they always receive wages much lower than those of the men.

Most women do not participate widely in farm activities; that is largely the men's sphere. When women do work, they tend to be employed in planting and the picking of cotton. Even when they work on their husbands' farms, they receive a wage.

Some women engage in trade and food processing for sale. Seclusion does not prohibit them from these activities. When seclusion restricts them from making some necessary contact with a supplier, children are utilised as a go-between. And women will perform a range of household chores for other people, in exchange for cash.

The role of women and some policy implications

The effect of seclusion on women is both good and detrimental. It tends to put a floor under their position, below which it cannot drop. The availability of land does mean that there is no landless class, and secluded women can be maintained. But it also puts a ceiling on the women's opportunities and horizons. Any project designed to raise the ceiling on secluded women's alternatives is also likely to lower the floor and that must be incorporated into the project. The class position of the family does affect the ability of the secluded woman to engage in income-generating activities and the return to those activities. This could have serious implications for any project designed to provide the secluded women with employment.

The sexual division of labour is well defined. Woman's work tends to be an extension of her household duties. The value placed on it is often not very high, and the growing taste for processed goods such as soft drinks and prepackaged foods may further lower the value of that work. Already, the returns to women's employment are less than the returns to men's (albeit an essentially universal phenomenon).

Planners must note that under the traditional division of labour and responsibilities, women will not necessarily benefit from an agricultural improvement programme just because men do. Men are under no obligation to pass on the fruits of the increased yield to women. Sometimes these male-oriented programmes may even harm the women's position. A fish-frying operation, set up and operated by men, cut into the market that was traditionally the women's.

Finally, it must be kept in mind that these observations may hold only for the village investigated. Areas vary in many respects. In this situation, it has been necessary to disaggregate the family, to determine who does what and receives what in the production process. In poorer areas, it may be that the family can be treated as a unit of production. Poverty forces all members of the family into farm work or employment. Seclusion of women is impossible where the women's contribution on the farm is necessary.

Conclusions and recommendations

In the case of the Wurinkada village, there are a number of
programmes and institutions that could help the women improve their
position and raise their horizons tremendously.   Formal credit
institutions could make loans directly available to women and
lessen their dependence on their men and male networks.   There is a
general need for the extension of rural health clinics to reduce the
time and energy involved in child care.   Possibly the women who
are past child-bearing age and who are not secluded could be used
to organise and introduce new activities for secluded women.   The
activities of women in the rural development project in the village
show that, despite their exclusion from it in every formal respect,
their informal networks and entrepreneurial skills enabled them to
become involved, and their conversion of resources to their use
further suggests that the form of resources provided to them is not
important as long as they are tradeable.

A basic needs strategy requires an injection of resources into
the woman's sphere as she provides many of these resources at a
family level.   Improvements are needed in her income-earning
capacity as well as in the domestic work she carries out for the
family.   The underutilisation of women's labour and expertise is
a constraint on development, and their current level of economic
activity suggests that they could become very effective entrepreneurs.

BIBLIOGRAPHY

Abdullah, A., and Zeidenstein, S.: Village Women of Bangladesh,
Prospects for Change. Study prepared for the ILO's World
Employment Programme (Oxford, Pergamon, 1982).

Beneria, L.; Reproduction, production and the sexual division of
labour, mimeographed World Employment Programme research
working paper; restricted (ILO, Geneva, 1978).

Hanger, J. and Moris, J.: "Women and the household economy", in
R. Chambers and J. Moris (eds.), Mwea: An Integrated Rice
Scheme in Kenya (Muhich, Welforum Verlag, 1973)

Haswell, M.R.: The changing pattern of economic activity in a
Gambia village, Overseas Research Publication 2 (UK Overseas
Development Administration, London, 1963).

Hill, P.: "Hidden trade in Hausaland", Man 4,3 (Sept. 1969),
pp. 392-409.

Hill, P.: Rural Hausa: A Village and a Setting (Cambridge
University Press, 1972)

Hill, P.: Population, Poverty and Prosperity (Cambridge University
Press, 1977)

Hill, P.: "Food-farming and migration from Fante villages",
Africa, 48,3 (1978), pp. 220-230.

Jackson, S., "Hausa women on strike", Review of African Political
Economy, 13 (1978), pp. 21-36.

Matlon, P.: The size distribution, structure and determinants of
personal income among farmers in the north of Nigeria,
Ph.D. Thesis (Cornell University, 1977).

Mernissi, F.: Beyond the Veil, J. Wiley and Sons, 1975.

Norman, D.W.: An economic survey of three villages in Zaria
Province, 2 Input-Output Vol. 1. Text. Samaru Miscellaneous
Paper 37 (Ahmadu Bello University, Nigeria, 1972)

Norman, D.W., Fine, J.C., Goddard, A.D., Kroeker, W.J. and
Pryor, D.H.: A Socio-Economic Survey of Three Villages in the
Sokoto Close-Settled Zone. 3 Input-Output Study, Vol. 1. Text.
Samaru Miscellaneous Paper 64 (Ahmadu Bello University,
Nigeria, 1976).

Simmons, E.B.: "The small-scale rural food processing industry in
northern Nigeria", Food Research Institute Studies,
Vol. XLV, 2 (1975), pp. 147-161.

Smith, M.G.: Baba of Karo (Faber and Faber, London, 1954).

Smith, M.G.: The Economy of Hausa Communities of Zaria, Colonial
Research Study 16, (HMSO, London, 1955).

Smith, M.G.: "The Hausa System of Social Status", Africa, XXIX, 3,
pp. 239-259 (1959).

Youssef, N.A.: "Education and Female Modernisation in the Muslim
World", Journal of International Affairs, 30, 2, pp. 191-209
(1976-77).

Chapter 8

CAPITALIST DEVELOPMENT AND PERCEPTIONS OF WOMEN
IN ARAB-MUSLIM SOCIETY: AN ILLUSTRATION OF
PEASANT WOMEN IN GHARB, MOROCCO*

by

Fatima Mernissi

Introduction

The purpose of this paper is to identify, for planners, ways
and means which will bring about rural modernisation while promoting
sexual and social equality.   It deals with questions such as:
what are the effects of the integration of the economy into the
international market on rural women, their participation and roles?
How does this integration affect the sexual division of labour and
the material and non-material gains received by individuals, men
and women? What are the effects of new technology on the condition
of rural women? In short, have technology and the integration of
the economy to the market improved or deteriorated the social and
sexual inequalities already existent in the precapitalist Moroccan
society?

The Gharb region was chosen for the study because more modernisation projects have taken place there.   The good quality of the land
and favourable weather conditions have given rise to capital
investment not only in the colonisation period but also after
independence.   In Gharb, one of the most successful programmes of
the colonisation took place - the allocation and transfer of land
to the colonialists which was accompanied by the transformation
of the production relations to the detriment of the subsistence
economy and in favour of much more market-oriented production.

This process was even reinforced after independence and the
programmes of rural development have favoured the integration of
agriculture in the international market with the concomitent
expansion of large production units at the expense of family units.

Poor rural women in Morocco work in a number of different
activities, yet they are not considered to be, by and large,
economic actors.   In the province of Gharb, Morocco, most of the
rural development programmes deal only with the activities of men.

_____

* French language original.

Development is considered to be a male phenomenon. This often means that women's lives become more difficult as planners, who do not take account of their "invisible" work, describe the area as improving. This paper attempts to examine this dichotomy from both a theoretical and a practical perspective. It begins with an exploration of the historical role and status of women in Arab-Muslim society, and then moves to a descriptive approach, examining the changes that have taken place in the lives of the women of Gharb. Finally, it makes some recommendations for improving their conditions and resolving the dichotomy between the perceptions of the planners and those of the women.

A historical perspective on the position of women in Arab-Muslim society

The first set of rules determining the sexual division of labour and the status of women is the set of rules found in the Koran. The Koran is very explicit about the different roles of the male and female. Men are considered the providers of the family; it is their responsibility to provide food, shelter, clothing and protection to the woman. In exchange, the woman is expected to fulfil a range of household duties, childbearing, child care, cooking, etc.

During the Golden Age of the Muslim Empire, the models of femininity of the Jariya, beautiful young slave girls, and the Houri, eternal virgins offered as a reward to those who achieve paradise, came to affect the perception of the role of the woman.

Then during the famine of the sixteenth and seventeenth centuries, hunger and poverty caused a huge upswing in the practice of slavery. Female slavery was particularly common and this practice lasted until the Second World War.

The introduction of technology and the wage labour economy under the colonists further affected the position of women on two levels. Manual labour was devalued with regard to new technological methods; and work for which one did not receive a wage was categorised as non-productive. Women were consistently relegated to non-remunerated manual labour, often in the domestic sphere. Thus, their work became less and less valuable in the local ideology. Women did not have the possibility of entering the market for "wage labour" because their productive and reproductive activities are controlled by men.

The nationalist movements of the 1930s added another aspect
to the perception of women's roles.   These movements called for
the abandonment of seclusion and the participation of the woman in
the economy, but participation along bourgeois lines.   Occupations
that were deemed proper for women were not accessible to at least
90 per cent of Moroccan women, who were not educated and not, by
and large, secluded.

Several ideologies have flourished since independence.   Many
of these exist side by side with new trends brought in from the
developed world through mass media, tourism and unemployment.   The
concept of the "dumb blonde" or the peasant woman as a dancer,
singer, entertainer have become more prominent through contact
with the West.

A consideration of the dynamics of sex roles and the perception
of feminine potential in the 1980s reveals a certain differentiation
among women.   One sees a dichotomisation of the female world in the
modern sector and the emergence of dominance and exploitation that
group maintains with the mass of women.   A female bourgeoisie
emerges through means of a diploma and salary, rupturing sex role
perceptions with consequences that could be determinant if they were
not based on class inequality.   Only the urban elite has access
to degrees and salaries and this has had the effect of an even
larger degradation of female manual workers in traditional sectors.

The case of Gharb

The traditional social structures based on family allegiances
provided a minimum of aid and protection to the women of Gharb.
They were guaranteed access to land although they were denied the
right to ownership.   They played a central part in the subsistence
economy, a part which was well recognised in the spiritual life of
the community.   This structure and the protection it provided
collapsed however with the extension of the market economy.

The new economy is based on large-scale agricultural holdings,
which hire only men, many of whom have been displaced from their
smallholdings.   The growth of large-scale holdings has further
reduced the size and availability of family holdings.   With no
improved technology, the woman's role has become harder to bear.
To provide for a family with constantly shrinking resources, she
must never cease working.   Even the improved status and comfortable
position of the elderly woman is denied to her in her old age, as
the pressure of poverty has fragmented the extended family.

Girls are needed to help their mothers at home and, thus, do not have the opportunity for education or training. The only release from the cycle of poverty, according to the women of Gharb, is the possibility of a wage-paying job. However, jobs are reserved for men only and women's work is based on the principle of non-remunerated labour.

The women know that they are living in need and they suggest three major areas in which they feel aid is most important: health and sanitation infrastructure; transportation, communication and education to relieve their isolation; and guaranteed employment.

Recommendations

Based on the theoretical exploration of the historical significance of women's roles and on the women's own perceptions of their needs, the author sets forth a series of recommendations to ameliorate the position of these women.

The abolition of the barrier between the public and the private sectors would allow the women to actually take part in new programmes. They would have access to new jobs and technology and would be able to participate in the development of their area more fully.

The size of agricultural enterprises should be regulated. They should be kept at a medium size, large enough to be productive, but small enough not to require the frequent aid of professionals and experts. Women should be allowed and encouraged to work alongside men on these holdings as equal partners.

The improvement of the transportation system and the ability of women to receive their own identity card would allow them greater freedom of movement. They would thus be able to seek work and to overcome some of their ignorance.

To achieve these reforms significant changes in attitudes toward women must take place. As a beginning all inequalities between men and women in the family law must be abolished and those who play an important role in shaping the future roles of rural women, planners, economists, statisticians, engineers and technicians, must be educated to understand the realities of women's work and the heavy burden on rural women.

BIBLIOGRAPHY

Adam, A.: Casablanca (Paris), 1972.

Al I man Malik Ibn Anas: Al Muwatta (Beyrouth, Dar Al Jadida), 1979.

Althusser, L.: Balibar, Lire le capital (Maspero), 1973.

Althusser, L.: "Idéologie et appareils idéologiques d'Etat", in Positions (Paris, Editions sociales), 1976.

Amin, K.: La libération de la femme (Egypt, Dar Al Maarit), 1880.

Basset, H.: Les rites du travail de la laine à Rabat (Rabat, Hesperis), 1922.

Boserup, E.: Women's role in economic development (New York, St. Martin's Press), 1974.

Bourderbala, N.: La question agraire au Maroc, Bulletin économique et social, no. triple 123-124-125, août), 1974.

Camilleri, C.: Jeunesse, famille et développement: essai sur le le changement socio-cultural dans un pays du tiers monde: Tunisie (Paris, CNRS), 1973.

Daily, M.: Gynecology (Boston, Beacon Press), 1978.

De Torres, D.: "Relation de l'origine et succès des chérifs ..." in Rosenberg and Tribi: Famines et épidémies au Maroc au 16ème et 17ème siècles (Rabat, Hesperis), 1973.

Dore, R.: The diploma disease (University of California Press), 1975.

Fanon, F.: "Mésaventure de la conscience nationale" et "Sur la culture nationale", in Les Damnés de la terre (Paris, Maspero), 1968.

Fassi, A.: Al harakat al istiglalia fi al maghrib al arib (Cairo), 1948.

_____: Autocritique (Beirut and Cairo), 1946.

Foucault, M.: Histoire de la sexualité, 1. La volonté de savoir (Paris, Gallimard), 1976.

Genovese, E.: The world the slaveholders made (New York, Random House), 1971.

Golvin, L.: Aspects de l'artisanat en Afrique du Nord (Presses Universitaires de France), p. 33, 1957.

Khaldoun, I.: Al mugaddimah Dar al kitab al arabi (Beirut), n.d.

Le Coz, Y.: Le Gharb, Fellahs et colons (Paris, CNRS), Vol. II, p. 431, 1964.

Le Coran: Essai d'interprétation du Coran inimitable (Paris, Gallimard) 892 pp., 1980.

"Les femmes dans la société" in Peuples, Vol. 7, No. 4.
Les Mille et une nuits (ed. 1980), p. 224.

Le Prévost, J.: El Glaoui (Paris), 1968.

Maher, V.: Women and property in Morocco (Cambridge University Press), 1974.

Marx, K.: Capital (New York, International Publishers), Vol. I, 1968.

Maxwell, G.: Lords of the Atlas (New York), 1966.

Meillassoux, C.: Femmes, greniers et capitaux (Paris, Maspero), 256 pp., 1975.

Mernissi, F.: "Les Bonnes" in Al Assas (Rabat), No. 5, 1977.

_____ : Le discours érotique religieux: réflexion sur les productions idéologiques dans l'islam dépendant (Paris, forthcoming).

_____ : Historical insights for new population strategies: Women in precolonial Morocco (Paris, UNESCO).

_____ : "Women's involvement in the saints and sanctuaries", in Journal of Women in Culture and Society, Vol. 3, No. 1, 1977.

_____ : "Le prolétariat féminin au Maroc", in Al Assas, 1980.

_____ : Le féminin, champ idéologique: Islam, classes, dépendance économique et création idéologique. Presented at the Round Table on "Les femmes et la division internationale du travail", Chantilly, 23-30 May 1980 (Paris), 1980.

Ministry of Agriculture and the Agrarian Reform: Statistiques agricoles: principales production végétales 1977-78 (Service des statistiques et de la documentation).

Pascon, P.: "Les grands moments de la caïdalité", in Le Haouz de Marrakech (NCRS, CVRS and Rabat), 1977.

Poulantzas, N.: Pouvoir politique et classes sociales (Paris, Maspero), 408 pp., 1982.

_____ : Classes sociales dans le capitalisme d'aujourd'hui (Paris, Seuil), 1974.

Rachid, A.: "Statut privé, règles, textes et explications", in Maktabat Ar-Rachad (Casablanca, Fès), 1965.

Rahman, A.: The 1919 revolution (Cairo), n.d.

Rodriguez: "Anais de Arzila", in Rosenberger et Tribi: Famines et épidémies au Maroc aux 16ème et 17ème siècles (Rabat, Hesperis), 1973.

Tizini, T.: Projet d'un nouveau regard sur le moyen âge musulman (Dar Dimashg) (in Arabic), 1971.

UNESCO: "Une école rurale à contenu axé sur les applications pratiques de la technologie", in Etude de cas socio-culturels, p. 25.

Zaidane, J.: Taris At-tamaddun Al Islami, Vol. V, p. 35.

Chapter 9

PARTICIPATION OF WOMEN IN RURAL DEVELOPMENT (NIGERIA)
by
Jadesola O. Akande

Introduction

The majority of the Nigerian population is rural dwelling and
engages in agriculture.   A number of crops are grown, but palm oil
and cocoa dominate the cash crop economy.   Most food and cash crops
are grown in the southern region, where this study was conducted.
The four States under examination are Oyo, Ogun, Ondo and Bendel.

In these four states, women are active participants in the
rural economy.   They are often farmers, working on land allocated
to their husbands or other male members of their families.   In
addition, they are usually responsible for the marketing of the farm
produce, and their importance as traders is reflected in the fact
that 50 per cent of the members of co-operatives and marketing
societies are women.   Many women also engage in handicrafts or
food production as commercial as well as subsistence activities.
Women rarely have only one occupation.

As much as women contribute to the rural economy, they have
not been integrated into rural development programmes in a way
commensurate with their economic roles.   The findings of this paper
corroborate the findings of other works concerning the integration
of women into rural development programmes.   Those programmes have
suffered from a lack of integration into the entire rural economy
and mode of production, and the image of the woman as a housewife
has contributed to that lack of integration.

Land tenure and agricultural policies

The land tenure system in southern Nigeria is still largely
based on communal land ownership.   Land is unalienable, and the
village head is responsible for overseeing its allocation.   Land
use is inherited patrilineally, but in cases of dispute, the village
head intervenes.   Land is regulated by the village head and the
village elders so that everyone who has need of it in order to
support a family has access to it.   However, men are usually the
only ones considered needy, and, thus, very little land is
allocated to women under this system.

This traditional land tenure system is gradually giving way to
a system of land ownership, which allows some women to own and

control land directly.   However, due to their lack of control over
capital and resources with which to buy land, women are still a small
minority of landowners.

The concept of family property, prevalent in Oyo, Ogun and Ondo
States, is that a piece of land belongs to a family through
generations for its use without belonging to any particular
individual member of the family.   Under this concept of family
property, the right of use can be conferred to women.   The one
disadvantage of this method of inheritance is that it can lead to
fragmentation of holdings into uneconomic units.   In Bendel
State the situation is different.   The system of inheritance
confers all family property on the first born son who is supposed to
hold the property in trust for the other children.   This system
dispossesses women of effective control of any land.   Agriculture
is becoming increasingly commercialised and the policy planners
seem to have assumed that all that is needed to raise agricultural
productivity is the consolidation of smallholdings and the introduction of mechanisation, which have further limited the amount
of land available to women.   Small plots often cultivated by
women have been appropriated and turned over to men, leaving women
with no alternative resources.

Mechanisation has also sharpened the division of labour.   Women
are not encouraged to go for training in the use of the new
machinery, which is considered only suitable for use by men.   They
tend to remain with their traditional and well-known implements,
which, although less efficient, give the women a sense of
participation in the production process, when they can still
participate.   In most of the cases, however, they are being
replaced by men and are being left with nothing, reverting to
a state of utter dependence when all they seem useful for is in the
kitchen.

At the moment, improved technology is not available to rural
women in any appreciable degree.   Where the Government has made
fertilisers available, men have dominated the distribution.   In
the area of food processing, laborious grinding of food which is
normally done by women is now done in some cases by machine.   In
one of the villages in Bendel State where a hydraulic palm oil
press was introduced, 72 per cent of the villagers used it, but
after a year the figure dropped to 24 per cent; the by-products
of the traditional processing method, the fibre used as a source

of heat, was lost; the daily time schedule for using the press did
not coincide with that of women; the machine, designed for men,
was difficult for the women to handle; finally, all oil extracted
belonged to men and the women did not benefit from the increase in
processed oil.

The integrated Rural Development Programme has set up programmes
for women who may be displaced from planting and harvesting because
of mechanisation.   However, they do not make any attempt to
integrate women into the rural development schemes, nor teach them
any skills that would allow them to participate in areas of the
economy outside of the domestic sphere.

In all the States, women's programmes are designed primarily
to teach women crafts and basic home economics.   The idea is that
women, through better home management, will be able to raise the
standard of living of their families, without any substantial capital
investment.

The ideology behind the rural extension services is that of
"separate but parallel development".   While men are taught new
agricultural skills and the management of new machinery, women
learn how to do what they always did, but better.

In the process of pursuing "separate" development, these
women's programmes ignore women's substantial role in the productivity
of the villages.

The programmes, in some cases, by failing to concentrate
resources on a level where the women have access to them, have
done very little to eradicate starvation and malnutrition.   In
some cases they have compounded them.   In one village in Ondo
State the agricultural reform programme took over the small plots
of land the women had relied on to feed their families.   Although
those women had participated in a training programme, they were
unable to feed their families or practice the skills they had
learned, for they had no land to farm and not enough income with
which to buy food and other essential goods.

Additionally, the programme of home economics deals mainly
with young married women.   The young unmarried women therefore
tend to migrate into urban settlements to become petty traders and/
or prostitutes.

Credit availability

Formal credit, where it is available in the rural areas, is not accessible to very poor families and to women in particular. Most women are not aware of the existence of formal credit insitutions, and high rates of female illiteracy prohibit them from making extensive use of them. In addition, there is a belief that without the support of men, there is no possibility of their being able to obtain credit.

Infrastructure

All over Nigeria there is a severe underdevelopment of infra-structure. Everybody suffers from the lack of educational facilities, health services, electrification, transportation and water supply. These shortages, however, are often more acute for women than for men, especially in the areas of education and transportation. Where women market produce, they must often carry it long distances to the market site on their heads. Some of these other shortages also directly affect the length and difficulty of the women's working day.

Women's organisations and groups in rural communities

In all the States investigated, there is a powerful tradition of voluntary women's groups. These groups are based on many things, age, religion, culture, or they may be traditional savings societies.   In all of the States women showed a tremendous ability to organise themselves and get things done.   In many areas women organised themselves into co-operative farming groups and pooled their plots. They created and maintained savings societies, and they built schools and other community buildings, often taking care of the organisation and staffing of the institutions as well. Traditionally women have been involved in co-operative trading and occasionally they handle the marketing of their husbands' farm products or are engaged in the procurement of some farm inputs.

Since there are groups based on so many characteristics, they often help unify the women. Age groups cut across class lines, and cultural groups cut across age and marital status lines. They thus provide a means by which women can identify common and community problems and actively attack them, and they also create a sense of solidarity among the women.

Conclusion

Rural development programmes in Nigeria have fallen far short of true integration of all members of the rural community into new and more efficient production systems. In many of these programmes it is women who have not received their share of assistance and aid. Programmes have, at times, increased rather than decreased their burden of work in the rural household. One of the major reasons they have failed to meet the women's needs has been a failure to incorporate them into the planning and design stages of the programmes. They have ignored the fact that women are producers, and that as essential producers they have important needs, which, when they are unmet, have dire consequences for the entire rural community. One of the most disappointing features of rural policy lies in the unhealthy assumption that all policies have to be formulated and written at the State's headquarters or by foreign experts.

Many rural women, though illiterate, are not unintelligent, and seeing their environment from their perspective would provide more acceptable solutions to their problems than the assumption that their problems are obvious. The hierarchy of decision-making in the rural household is still very much against women. The men still make all the important decisions and roles are not inter-changeable under any circumstances.

The lack of infrastructure and credit facilities, and the restriction on the resources available to most women create a vicious circle, in which women are unable to break out of their disadvantaged position. A great deal of work still needs to be done, with the women themselves, teaching them new skills and raising their economic and ideological horizons, with the community, educating it to accept women in all stages of production, in the provision of employment, resources and technical aid, and with the planners, educating them to the fact that the rural situation is not as simple as it looks to them. The programme of separate but parallel development has been proven ineffective in the rural community, for it has failed to realise that there is a complex set of relationships between the tasks that must be accomplished, the individuals who perform them and the distribution of rewards. It has failed to listen to the people themselves, particularly the

women, about what needs to be done and what will not work. The
voluntary women's organisations, which have been so successful in
identifying the needs of rural people, and meeting those needs, are
a promising place to start. Because of their diverse nature, they
could provide both information and action in many different areas
on many different kinds of problems. Perhaps, most importantly,
they can provide a means for including the women in the design and
decision-making stages of rural development projects.

BIBLIOGRAPHY

Abell, H.A.:   Socio-economic Survey of Peasant Agriculture in
     Northern Nigeria (FAO, Rome) 1962.

Adegboye, R.O.: "The Need for Land Reform in Nigeria",
     Nigerian Journal of Economic and Social Studies, Vol. 9,
     No. 3, 1964.

Ahmed, Z.: "The Plight of Rural Women: alternatives for action",
     International Labour Review,Vol. 119, No. 4 1980.

Boserup, E.: Women's Role in Economic Development (New York
     St. Martins Press) 1970.

Di Domenico, C.M. and L.: Lacey - Mojuetan, "Occupational Status
     of Women in Nigeria: A Comparison of Two Urban Centres",
     paper presented at the Conference on Nigerian Women and
     Development in Relation to Changing Family Structure,
     26-30 April (Department of Sociology, University of Ibadan,
     Nigeria, pp. 3-15), 1976.

Ladipo, P.: "Modernisation of the Traditional Labour Force:
     Prerequisite or Determinant to Development" reports that
     less than 10 per cent of such equipments are owned by women
     even in such big urban centres as Ibadan and Ife.

Ministry of Local Government (Community Development Division),
     Community Development in Bendel State.

Ministry of Economic Planning, Rural Agricultural Survey in the
     Oyo State of Nigeria (Statistics Division, Ibadan,
     Oyo State of Nigeria), 1978.

Nigeria: Third National Development Plan.

Oluwasanmi, H.A.: "Agriculture in a Developing Economy",
     Journal of Agricultural Economics, 1964.

Patel, A.U. and Q.B.O. Anthonio: Farmers' Wives in Agricultural
     Development: The Nigerian Case (Department of Agricultural
     Economics and Extension, University of Ibadan, Nigeria), 1973.

UNECA: Women in the Traditional and Modern Labour Force,
     Africa Training and Research Centre for Women, 1976.

Chapter 10

RURAL WOMEN IN A RESETTLEMENT PROJECT:
THE CASE OF THE LIBYAN ARAB JAMAHIRIYA
by
Farida Allaghi

Introduction

This research is an attempt to explore a case study in the
Libyan Arab Jamahiriya, where an educational programme in the
Kufra Settlement Project (KSP) was created, and to find out if this
programme is indeed having an impact on the decision-making involvement of the participants within their families.   The main goal of
the Kufra Settlement Project is to establish settlements with
integrated services to secure the stability of farmers and their
families in their new society and to encourage them not to migrate
to the cities.   One of the objectives of the KSP is to improve
the lifestyle of women.   The new homes with all needed services
such as water, electricity and sanitation are among many other
mechanisms that have been established by the Government of the
Libyan Arab Jamahiriya to achieve this goal.   The major mechanism,
however, as conceived by the resettled women is the Rural Women's
Development Centre (RWDC).   In this RWDC women are primarily
trained in home economics skills (cooking, sewing, knitting,
embroidery) and are taught how to read and write.   The training
programme lasts nine months.   The presence or absence of women's
participatory roles in decision-making within their families is an
indicator of whether or not the development process is positively
benefiting women, especially by increasing their power and status,
which affects their participatory capabilities in their families'
decisions.   Bearing this relationship in mind between development
and women's effective participation in decision-making, inquiry on
women's participation in the development processes would constitute
an inquiry on their participation in their family's decision-making.
In looking at women's education in the Rural Development Centre at
the Kufra Settlement Project, the study attempts to test the major
hypothesis which is: the more extensive the utilisation of the
skills learned at the centre in the home by the daughters, the more
is the daughter's effective involvement in the decision-making
pattern of the family.   By testing this general hypothesis in this
case study, the findings will contribute to our knowledge about the

overall impact of development projects on rural women's general
well-being.

The Libyan context

The country has a severe manpower shortage and suffers from a
great and growing dependence on foreign workers.   Yet, according
to the census date, 94.8 per cent of Libyan women are unemployed.
This huge reserve of women could, if activated, make a tremendous
difference in the national labour situation.   The Government has
taken some steps to attract women into the labour force, and
theoretically, all workers both male and female, are entitled to
the same rights.   There is widespread recognition of the need for
Libyan women to participate in the labour force.   However, cultural
norms and existing social and economic institutions still prohibit
this from occurring.

Education is one area in which the inequalities between men and
women effectively limit the ability of women to participate on equal
footing with men.   The Government's education plan promises to
provide separate education for girls, whenever possible, as an
encouragement to women's education in a traditional and conservative
culture.   However, a shortage of trained and qualified teachers,
funds and facilities, often means that only the men and boys receive
adequate education.

The Kufra Resettlement Project

The Kufra Resettlement Project is situated in the Sahara Desert
on the Kufra Oasis.   Agriculture in this region is impossible without extensive irrigation.   At its completion, the project intends
to have space for 4,500 people, organised into 55 hamlets of 16
farms each.

The goals of the resettlement programme are to increase the
self-sufficiency capabilities of the country, to protect its resources and to improve the standard of living of a large segment of
the population.

Most of the families on the project come from scattered oases
in the Sahara.   The women's old lifestyle included housework,
shepherding, water collecting and farm work.   Some of the women also
engaged in schlef, a form of rug weaving with homespun wool, or
basketweaving.   Women were very active in the economic lives of

their families and communities, although their standard of living
was very low.   Homes were dirty and unhealthy and there was a
complete lack of physical and social infrastructure.   In the new
project area, household duties are easy and do not demand too much
time, farm work is done mainly by men, under the supervision of
technical advisers and with the aid of imported machinery.   Schlef
and basketweaving are impossible without the raw materials, which
are no longer available.   Water does not need to be collected, nor
sheep herded.   Women's activities have been reduced to housekeeping,
and, in the new houses with modern conveniences, that is not a very
demanding role.   Despite the positive general attitude towards
women's formal education and work outside the house, the women's
opportunities at the project site are very limited.   There is a
formal female school under construction, but in the meanwhile the
only educational opportunity for women is the Rural Women's
Development Centre (RWDC).   This Centre runs a nine-month training
course for women, to teach them home economics and skills, like
sewing and knitting.   No education in areas such as reading and
writing is available to women on the project, and no job opportunities
after the training.

Although everyone interviewed liked the RWCD programme, many
felt it did not go far enough and was not comprehensive enough.
The women's programme clearly reflects the middle-class bias of the
planners, who did not perceive a role for women that went beyond
that of the housewife.   The important incentives this study finds
among the people of the Kufra project, both women and men, for the
women to work both inside and outside the household, are ignored in
the design of the women's role at Kufra.

Major findings

Concerning the testing of the general hypothesis of the study, a
weak and negative relationship was found between the daughter's
involvement in family decision-making and the daughter's utilisation at home of the skills learned at the Centre.   Even when controlling for education, age or family size, although some different
reactions were observed, the general findings did not change
significantly.   These results lead to the initial conclusion that
the RWDC may not have made any difference concerning involvement of
daughters in family decision-making.   Settling women in new
projects may be necessary for improving their and their families'
standard of living, but it is not sufficient to ensure their total

development.   While large-scale economic and materialistic changes
have occurred at the KSP, the needed changes in the traditional
lifestyle and changes in social structure did not occur.   Many
deep-rooted cultural attitudes concerning women persisted.
Obviously the external environment of women at KSP has been transformed, but the internal pattern of family life appears to proceed
as before.   However, one could not imply that the process of
development has been totally negative for women, as part of the
literature implies.

This case study also shows what has already been emphasised
by many other researchers in the area of women, that women's role
and status in societies should not be dealt with as a separate
issue, but should rather be considered as an integral part of the
overall issue of rural and national development.   The mere
creation of the RWDC without a supporting infrastructure in the
project as a whole did not truly help women to benefit completely
from development.

There is no opportunity for the women to market what they have
learned; the facilities they need to do that are not available. For
example, there is only limited use for the products women knit and
sew at the Kufra oasis, where the weather is hot most of the year.
At the same time, they have no facilities for transporting and
marketing the goods in cities where it gets cold enough for there
to be a need for warm garments.   The sewing machines that women
are given on graduation from the Centre eventually break, but there
is no one at the project site who knows how to fix them.

The RWDC does not teach any skills outside of home economics
and handicrafts.   Thus, there are no new activities it allows women
to become involved in, and it does not help them break out of their
traditional roles.   A course in basic reading and writing was
dropped from the syllabus, and, although the syllabus does list agricultural training as part of the offerings, it is not actually
offered.

On the project site, there are no job opportunities open to
women.   A few women help out on their fathers' farms, but that
practice is neither widespread nor full time.   There are no shops
or effective communication with the surrounding area.   Many of the
women had expected to find some provision made for their employment
when they came to the resettlement project, and they felt considerable disappointment on discovering that they had been almost

completely overlooked in the project design.   The RWDC does very
little toward training the women in marketable skills or skills that
might provide them with a viable alternative economic role on the
project site.

This study did uncover the significant fact that the major
barrier to women's employment is not, as many of the programme planners
believe, the inflexibility of the traditional household structure,
or the hard headedness of the people, but it is the lack of job
opportunities for women.   This study finds that the majority of men
were willing to have their wives or daughter work outside the home,
particularly in occupations considered to be the domain of women,
some of which carry quite a high status.

Recommendations

The programmes that have been and still are created in most of
the developing countries, including the Libyan Arab Jamahiriya,
which aim to deal with women's problems reflect the perception of
the planners, who are usually urban middle or upper class.   These
planners in essence developed a model of housewifery for solving
women's problems.   They believe that helping women means only
shunting them into handicrafts or programmes for cooking and
nutrition.   This misleading notion has hindered the creation of
other programmes which might give women productive skills, open new
work opportunities, and ensure their economic independence.   There
is a great deal to be done both on the level of the national programme of development and at the Kufra project site, in order to
integrate women more fully into rural development.   It should
be pointed out that in a country such as the Libyan Arab
Jamahiriya where the lack of trained human resources and labour
force are listed by the government planners as being major
obstacles facing the implementation of various developmental
projects, any call for educating women and training them should
not be a debatable or neglected issue among the planners.   If
these women are not trained in order to participate in the
modernisation process, their human resources that are needed for
the country's development could be partially going to waste.

At the Kufra project, there are a number of steps that could
be taken to channel women's energy and abilities into productive
activities.   These steps could also improve the women's position
vis-à-vis the community and improve the standard of living on the
whole project.

Changes at Kufra must begin with dramatic attitudinal change.
Men, women and planners must accept that women have economic
potential.   Planners in particular must realise that there is not
as much opposition to women working as the design of their programmes expect.

The kinds of skills that the RWDC teaches have got to be integrated and economically viable, and support systems, such as transportation and credit institutions, should be set up to allow the
women to make them so.   Some marketable skills should be included
in the curriculum.

The area of training has got to be expanded to include literacy
training.   There should be some attempt to include education about
issues touching the women's lives.

The group of students the Centre draws from could be widened to
include more women, and the facilities must be increased to handle
the new students and parts of the curriculum.   The training period
must be increased to enable new programmes to be at all valuable.

Finally, leadership skills could be developed among the women,
to make them capable of running their own programme, and new, more
efficient management techniques could make a huge difference in the
organisation of the Centre.

On the national level, the development programmes suffer from
some serious weaknesses.   Women's programmes must be incorporated
into the Government ministeries and existing institutions.   Social
and institutional structures must be modified to allow women to
fully participate in all aspects of social and economic life.
Government planners must learn about the activities and roles of
people they are dealing with, especially the invisible activities
of rural women.   National women's organisations must take active
roles in rural development.   Women themselves must actively participate in programmes wherever they can, and they must take an active
part in the founding and management of their own organisations.
Finally, development programmes must be, at least in the beginning,
welfare oriented, for there is still such a long way to go, that
immediate aid is necessary before the programmes can begin to be
self-sustaining or generate a return.

BIBLIOGRAPHY

Alfahum, Siba: The Libyan Woman, 1965-1975 (Beirut: Lebanese
    Section, Women's International League for Peace and
    Freedom, 1977).

Al-Huni, Ali Mohamed: Determinants of Female Labour Force
    Participation: The Case of Libya (Pennsylvania: University
    of Pittsburg, unpublished dissertation in economics, 1979).

Allaghi, Farida: The Libyan Woman in Transition (Fort Collins,
    Colo.: Colorado State University, unpublished M.A. thesis
    in sociology, 1973).

Allaghi, Farida and Zakiya El-Sahli: On Libyan Women. The Mission
    of Libya to the United Nations Organisation, Paper No. 8,
    (1978).

Beck, Lois and Nikkie Keddie (Eds.): Women in the Muslim World.
    (Cambridge, Mass.: Harvard University Press, 1978).

Blumberg, Rae Lesser: "Fairy Tales and Facts: Economy, Family,
    Fertility, and the Female". In Women and World Development,
    Irene Tinker and Michele Bo Bramsen (eds.) (New York:
    Praeger Publishers, 1976), pp. 12-21.

Boserup, Ester: Women's Role in Economic Development (New York:
    St. Martin's Press, 1970)

Boulding, Elise: Women in the Twentieth Century World. Studies
    on Women and Development (Boulder, Colo.: Sage
    Publications, 1977).

    The Underside of History. A View of Women through Time.
    (Boulder, Colo.: Westview Press, 1976).

Buvinic, Mayra: Women and World Development. An annotated
    bibliography. (Washington, DC.: Overseas Development
    Council, 1976)

Cromwell, E., Ronald and Stephen G. Wieting: "Multidimensionality
    of Conjugal Decision-making Indices: Comparative Analysis
    of Five Samples". Journal of Comparative Family Studies,
    Vol. 6, No. 2 (Autumn, 1975): pp. 139-151.

Darrat, Ibraheem: On Libya and Foreign Aid. New York: The
    Mission of Libya to the United Nations Organisation.
    Paper No. 3 (1978).

    On Libya and the United Nations Development Programme.
    New York: The Mission of Libya to the United Nations
    Organisation. Paper No. 4 (1979).

Delegation of Libya to the United Nations Commission on the
    Status of Women: Report on the Libyan Woman (New York, 1978).

Dixon, Ruth: Rural Women at Work: Strategies for Development in
    South Asia (Baltimore, Johns Hopkins Press, 1978).

Ekejiuba, Felicia Ifeona: "Women and Symbolic Systems Introduction". In Women and National Development: The Complexities of Change. Wellesley Editorial Committee (Chicago, The University of Chicago Press, 1977) pp. 90-92.

El Maihub, Saleh: Investment in a Capital Surplus Country: The Case of Libya (Fort Collins, Colo., Colorado State University, unpublished Ph.D. dissertation in economics, 1977).

First, Ruth: Libya: The Elusive Revolution (New York, African Publishing Company, 1975).

Giele, Janet Sollinger and Audrey Chapman Smock: Women's Roles and Status in Eight Countries (New York, John Wiley and Sons, Inc., 1977).

Higgins, Benjamin Howard: The Economic and Social Development of Libya (New York, United Nations, 1953).

Huston, Perdita: Third World Women Speak Out: Interviews in Six Countries on Change, Development, and Basic Needs (published in co-operation with the Overseas Development Council, 1978).

Joyce, M. Lynda and Samuel M. Leadley: An Assessment of Research Needs of Women in the Rural United States: Literature Review and Annotated Bibliography (Pennsylvania State University: Department of Agricultural Economics and Rural Sociology, 1977).

Libyan Arab Republic: Primary Results of the 1974 General Census (Ministry of Planning, Division of Statistics and Census).

Population Provision until 1985. Tripoli (Ministry of Planning, Demography and Manpower Division).

The Three-year Economic and Social Development Plan, 1973-1975. Tripoli (Ministry of Planning).

Libyan Arab Republic Council of Land Reclamation and Reconstruction: Women and the Agricultural Revolution in the Country. Tripoli: The Executive Board of Jefara Region, Eljalaa Press (1977).

Maklouf, Carle: Changing Veils: Women and Modernization in North Yemen (Austin, University of Texas Press, 1979).

Mason, John P.: "Sex and Symbol in the Treatment of Women in the Wedding Rite in a Libyan Oasis Community". American Ethnologist, Vol. 2, No. 4 (November 1975), pp. 649-661.

Mead, Richard and Alan George: "The Women of Libya". Middle East International, July, pp. 18-20 (1973).

Mernissi, Fatima: Country Report on Women in the North African Countries: Morocco, Libya, Tunisia. Addis Ababa (United Nations Economic Commission for Africa, 1975).

Mickelwait, R. Donald, Mary Ann Riegleman and Charles F. Sweet: Women in Rural Development: A Survey of the Roles of Women in Ghana, Lesotho, Kenya, Nigeria, Bolivia, Paraguay and Peru (Boulder, Colo., Westview Press, 1976).

Murphy, Ernest Nancy Sadke and Nadia Youssef: An Evaluation of Non-formal Education Programs for Women in Morocco: A Joint Report for the Agency of International Development (Washington, DC., 1977).

Nash, June: Certain Aspects of the Integration of Women in the
    Development Process: A Point of View (New York, United Nations
    World Conference of the International Women's Year.
    E/Conf. 66/BP/5, 1975).

Nelson, Cynthia: Public and Private Politics: Women in the
    Middle Eastern World, the Ethnographic Image (Cairo, The
    American University).

Rodman, Hyman: "Marital Power and the Theory of Resources in the
    Cultural Context". Journal of Comparative Family Studies,
    Vol. 3, No. 1 (Spring, 1972) pp. 59-69.

Safilios, Rothschild: "The Study of Family and Power Structure:
    A Review, 1960-1969". Journal of Marriage and Family,
    Vol. 32, No. 4 (1970).

Stoler, Ann: Land, Labor and Female Autonomy in a Javanese Village
    (Columbia University, Department of Anthropology, 1975).

Subcommittee on Women in Development of the Committee on
    Development Assistance: Criteria for Evaluation of
    Development Projects Involving Women. New York: Technical
    Assistance Clearing House (American Council of Voluntary
    Agencies for Foreign Service, 1975).

Sudarkasa, Niare: "Women and Migration in Contemporary West
    Africa". In Women and National Development: The
    Complexities of Change (Chicago, Wellesley Editorial
    Committee, the University of Chicago Press, 1977), pp. 178-189.

Tinker, Irene and Michele Bo Bramsen (Eds.): Women and World
    Development (Washington, DC.: Overseas Development
    Council, 1976).

Tryfan, Barbara: The Role of Rural Women in the Family (Baton
    Rouge, La.: unpublished paper presented at the Third World
    Congress of Rural Sociology, 1972).

United Nations Economic Commission for Africa: the Data Base for
    Discussion of the Interrelations between the Integration
    of Women in Development, their Situation and Population
    Factors in Africa (New York: UN Doc. E/CN.14/SW/17, 1974).

United Nations World Conference of the International Women's Year:
    Current Trends and Changes in the Status and Roles of Women
    and Men and Major Obstacles to be Overcome in the Achievement
    of Equal Rights Opportunities and Responsibilities
    (New York, E/CONF:6613/Add.1, 1975).

United Nations World Plan of Action: Decade for Women (New York,
    United Nations, 1975).

Vlachos, Evan: Human Resource in Rural Development. Problems
    of Integration in Libyan Rural Settlements. Preliminary
    proposal submitted to the Council of Agricultural Development,
    Libya (Fort Collins, Colo., Department of Sociology,
    Colorado State University, 1977)

Wright, John: Libya (New York, Frederick A. Praeger Publishers,
    1969).

Chapter 11

A SURVEY OF AFRICAN WOMEN PETTY TRADERS AND SELF-EMPLOYED IN TOWN AND COUNTRY IN SOUTH AFRICA

by

Daphne Sbongile Nene

Introduction

Rural women, as people who have traditionally engaged in domestic activities that accommodate the provisioning role without domestic stress, are now faced with new challenges in the modern sector as they have to balance the demands made on them by employment outside of their family circle on the one hand, and keeping families together, on the other.

These women occupy the lowest socio-economic strata of their society, as they suffer limitations not only because of their geographical setting, but also because of the added sex discrimination in the job market. Often isolated into particular "women's" categories of a temporary or seasonal nature, they lack the opportunity to develop in the job and to master a wider range of skills.

The research is focused upon a previously undocumented facet of the rural economy of KwaZulu - that of the activities of rural women engaged in petty trading. Although the subjects of the study are rural born and bred and maintain their role in the peasant agriculture of the area, they have simultaneously expanded their economic horizons by taking advantage of growing markets for food products, both raw and cooked, and for handicrafts, provided firstly by the busy national highway to the north and secondly by the growth of Empangeni, a middle-sized town where few facilities are offered to Blacks for food and drink. The money-making activities of these women - often referred to as making up part of the "informal sector" - are focused, therefore, firstly upon specialist trade to passing White tourists in indigenous clay pots, mats and beadwork, secondly upon the provision of basic foodstuffs such as fresh fruit and vegetables which are sold both to Whites and to the Black locals and travellers, and thirdly upon the provision of cooked snacks and home brewed liquor for which there is a great demand amongst Blacks visiting the centre of Empangeni.

In South Africa, their problems are particularly acute, for the environment is openly hostile. The White zones in which the women petty traders operate are both legally and economically

foreign terrain.   The four areas which this study encompasses all
have their differences, in terms of the marketing patterns and
strategies.   However, the women all share the experience of being
outsiders - racially, sexually and economically - and they share a
spectrum of problems that go along with that status.

The four areas in which fieldwork was done are described briefly
below.   Although they differ dramatically in the type and frequency
of trading engaged in and the markets catered to, they are all
within the same general geographical area.   Some of the similarities
in the marketing processes and the problems are then drawn out,
followed by some common attitudes toward the women's work.
Finally, a programme is designed, through which the author believes
the problems can be attacked.

Areas of fieldwork

Macekane I is an extremely isolated rural area.   The women
engage in organised poultry and vegetable farming, under the direction of a peace corps volunteer.   Their marketing activities are
extremely limited; of the 90 women involved in the poultry farming
project, only 10 participated in petty trading, about once a month.
Trading involves buying fruits, vegetables and poultry at a local
level or using their own surplus, and transporting it in trucks to
a township 8 km away.   The women then move from house to house in
groups of four to five, for fear of being robbed, and because the
dominant ideology in their isolated rural area prohibits women from
acting alone and independently.   They are afraid of being labelled
"cheap".

The second area has been exposed to a much greater "modern"
influence.   It is located along the Kwa-Dlangezwa Highway, near the
University of Zululand.   The cash needs of these people, to pay for
school fees and necessary supplies, are greater than those of the
Macekane I people, who are practically self-sufficient.   These
traders are mostly dependent on male suppliers, who sell them fresh
produce, often bought from White farmers.   The cost of these products is high, as the women depend almost entirely on middlemen to
provide them with the produce and transportation.   A few vendors
also sell produce from their own gardens.   Most of the produce is
raw and perishable.   Thus, the women are unable to buy in bulk and
reduce costs.   The clientele is largely made up of tourists and
hunters on their way north to the game reserves; locals rarely buy

from these vendors because their prices are beyond the local prices.
Profits, therefore, vary with the tourist trade.

The Obanjeni Highway sellers are somewhat more isolated than
the Kwa-Dlangezwa people, but they have many of the same cash needs.
They market more handicrafts than food, and must deal with problems
of breakage and storage.   Pottery is their most common good,
although they also market basketry, grass mats and some beadwork.
They used to store their goods by hiding them in sugar-cane fields
near the highway, but breakage and robbery were common.   More
recently they have been using a protected spot outside of a local
store, with the permission of the White store owner.   Storage is
still a big problem, and stockpiling of goods is impossible.

These women show the greatest tendency toward organisation.
Pots are ordered from women further inland, and about once a month a
group of women will hire a truck to pick up the pots.   The women
all demonstrated a sense of commitment to and dependence on each
other.

The last group under study is the bus rank vendors in the urban
area of Empangeni.   These women face problems of the same type, but
on a much greater scale than the other groups of traders.   Their
biggest problem is that of police raids.   Empangeni is White-owned
and controlled.   These women engage in trade that is considered
illegal.   Police will raid them up to three times a week destroy
or confiscate their stock and sometimes arrest or fine them.   They
sell anything they can, handicrafts, produce, poultry and cooked
goods.   Their stock rarely amounts to very much as they have problems with storage, transport, raids and lack of capital.   They sell
their goods under the most unhygienic of conditions, in open display
containers, exposed to dust and weather.   Most of the traders live
in the areas around the city, covering between 4 and 40 km to reach
the market site.

Again, many traders are dependent on middlemen to provide
them with their stock.   A few grow or cook their own stock.   Their
dependence on middlemen, and the fact that they can only buy a
little at a time, mean that they must pay high prices for the goods
they sell.

Common marketing patterns and problems

A few of the common problems are obvious from this brief description of the areas studied.   Many of the problems stem from a

lack of organisation among the women, given the sociological
environment under which they operate, the legal constraints, the
isolation from mainstream big business or entrepreneurial skills
and generally low literacy levels, dependence on middlemen to
provide and transport goods and the inability to buy in bulk raise
the cost of the products to the women, thereby cutting into their
profits. The fact that these women are isolated, operate alone
in a hostile environment and lack formal, and often even informal,
support mechanisms, means that they are particularly vulnerable
to exploitation and crisis, such as the police raids. They
also lack access to technical expertise on profitable marketing
techniques. They often repeat activities individually that could
be done once for the whole group, wasting time, energy and often
cash on such things as transportation.

Many other problems are a result of a lack of infrastructure.
Storage is often a problem in its own right. Food and handicrafts
are often ruined from exposure to the weather and dirt. Transportation is a major problem, especially for the urban bus rank sellers.
Where it is available, it is expensive, sometimes prohibitively so.
The lack of education and high rate of illiteracy mean that the
women cannot take advantage of Black commerce organisations, in the
cases where they exist.

Petty trading is a very time-consuming occupation, with a very
low rate of return. Profitability is variable, usually low, so no
fixed-income can be depended on. Under these conditions capital
accumulation is very difficult and there is not much chance for
improvement of capital resources.

The single greatest obstacle to all these women is their low
and illegal status. There is no way that they can form legal
organisations or take advantage of protective legislation, for the
law does not recognise what they do as valid. There are no government programmes to ameliorate their condition. In fact, there are
no programmes to deal with their problems at all. The women's
legal status remains unchanged, they are minors. The burden they
carry is in no way commensurate with the status of minor. Looking
after the interests of the household on the one hand, they struggle
to retain a modicum of decency and self-respect in a society that
has, actively and inadvertently, degraded their position, on the
other.

Economic need and ambitions

South Africa has been undergoing a demographic shift that has left more and more rural women in positions of financial responsibility for their families. Male migration in search of work is heavy and growing. Black male unemployment is high everywhere, but especially so in the rural areas. The combination of higher life expectancy for women and the tendency for them to marry older men means there are many widows. Growing and deepening destitution weaken the ability of the extended family system to take in and provide for deserted, divorced or widowed women. The women who find themselves victims of these trends are usually the ones who turn to petty trading.

Petty traders who are unmarried mothers, widows, wives of unemployed or underemployed men, wives whose husbands have migrated in search of employment and deserted wives, must often provide for numerous dependents. Most of the petty traders in this category have large families, and their incomes are necessary for the support of those families. In an economy that increasingly demands cash for commodities and education, petty trading is becoming not less, but more important as an income-generating activity.

The most outstanding feature is their high hopes for a better future for themselves and their families. Seventy per cent of the women wish to extend their economic activities by being able to buy larger stock, have a better marketing system, form an organisation and invest money in a bank or commercial activity. Opening up a business of their own is a dream shared by a few. Women are in need of proper trading permits as they do not have them.

All the women interviewed in the study expressed a concern for their families and the hope that their children would be able to find a better way of life. All the women have high aspirations for their children irrespective of sex. Only 2 per cent regarded secondary school education as adequate for their children's careers, while high school coupled with a profession was preferred by 45 per cent of the women. Forty per cent were desirous of university education for children. Given all the hardships, the long hours, insecurity and low return of petty trading, the women continue to engage in it because to them it is the only means of support and the only means through which the next generation will be able to survive and make its own attempt at improvement. The sense of responsibility to their families, particularly the children,

and the feeling that there are few alternative activities that could
meet their needs are evident in the doggedness with which they toil
in unhealthy surroundings, exposed to all sorts of weather.   They
all plead need.   Their families would starve if they did not
continue.

Strategies to deal with the plight of
the petty traders

In the context of the dual South African society, it is clear
that any strategy to improve the conditions of the petty traders
must be total.   It must include programmes to aid the women themselves, providing them with the necessary infrastructure to continue
trade, protection, technical and legal assistance, credit and bank-
ing facilities and programmes through which they can buy at reduced
or perhaps wholesale rates.   It must also include, however, a programme of education aimed at the population at large.   People must
learn to accept the concept of Black, female traders as valid economic
actors, with valid economic needs.

These programmes, however, cannot be provided formally without
a re-evaluation and change of the country's legal code.   As long
as petty trading is illegal in White South Africa, infrastructure
and education will have to be provided in an informal manner.   The
author suggests a programme of small-scale, informal organisation
to begin with, perhaps three or four women.   These, should grow
into small petty traders' organisations to provide advice, technical
aid, deal with police, promote co-operation, eventually leading to
the development of resource and credit centres.   Stress in all
these stages should be on organisation and co-operation.

Eventually, with enough resources amassed, a programme of
public symposia and consultation networks could be launched to promote the women's own awareness of their exploitation and their need
for better organisation.   Education programmes could begin to alert
both the public and the authorities to the economic needs of the
women.   Organisations of this type could also allow the effective
use of pressure for legal change.

Conclusion

Many of the solutions to the problems described in this report are achievable only through dramatic <u>social</u> change. The women live under increasingly heavy economic and social pressures. They are forced to take an active and responsible economic role, yet they live in a society that does not recognise their needs and their attempts to fill that role. Outmoded ideas of the woman's proper role and sexual prejudices are obstacles they share with all women forced into roles of economic responsibility. Racial prejudice locks them into a position of subservience. It is important to remember that most of these women do not perceive a choice in their activities. It is need that dictates the activities of these South African petty traders.

BIBLIOGRAPHY

Boserup, E.: Women's Role in Economic Development (St. Martin's Press, New York, 1970).

Bryant, A.T.: The Zulu People (Shuter & Shooter, Pietermaritzburg, 1949).

Clarke, L. and Ngobese, T.: Women without Men (Black Research, Durban, 1975).

Hunter, M.: Reaction to Conquest (Oxford University Press, 1961).

Krige, E.: The Social System of the Zulus (Shuter & Shooter, Pietermaritzburg, 1965).

Little, K.: African Women in Towns (Cambridge University Press, 1973)

Longmore, L.: The Dispossessed. A study of sex life of Bantu women in urban areas, in and around Johannesburg (Johathan Cape, London).

Mayer, P.: Townsmen or Tribesmen (Oxford University Press, 1963).

Nattrass, J.: Migrant Labour and Underdevelopment. The Case of Kwa Zulu (University of Natal, Durban, 1977).

Nkabinde, C.: "The Legal Position of African Women in Employment", IPST Bulletin, Vol. 12, pp. 27-32 (University of Zululand, 1978).

Preston-Whyte, E.M.: "The making of a Townswoman: The Process and Dilemma of Rural Urban Migration Amongst African Women in Southern Natal". Sociology, Southern Africa, Durban (University of Natal, 1973).

"Families without Marriage: A Zulu Caste Study". In W. Argyle and E. Preston-Whyte (eds.) Social System and Tradition in Southern Africa (Capetown, Oxford University Press, 1978).

Rip, C.: Contemporary Social Pathology (University of Pretoria, 1966).

Schapera, I.(ed.): The Bantu Speaking Tribes of South Africa (London, Routledge, 1937).

Thorrington-Smith: Towards a Plan for Kwa Zulu (1978).

Turner, N.: "Matrifocality" in M. Rosaldo and Lamphere (eds.), Woman, Culture and Society (Stanford University Press, 1974).

Tripartite African Regional Seminar
on Rural Development and Women
Dakar, 15-19 June 1981

––––––––––

Séminaire Régional Tripartite pour l'Afrique
sur le Développement Rural et la Femme
Dakar, 15-19 juin 1981

LIST OF PARTICIPANTS/
LISTE DES PARTICIPANTS

Iqbal AHMED	Adviser-Employment and Development Policy, SATEP, ILO, Lusaka, Zambia
Vanda ALTARELLI HERZOG	Independent Researcher, Freelance Consultant
Anna BATHILY	WID (Women in Development) Officer, USAID, Dakar, Sénégal
Danielle BAZIN	ILO Regional Office for Africa, PO Box 2788, Addis Ababa, Ethiopia
Alain BRAUD-MENSAH	Administrateur, Association Interprofessionelle des employeurs de Côte d'Ivoire 01, BP 1340, Abidjan PO, Côte d'Ivoire
Eugenia DATE-BAH	Technology and Employment Branch, Employment and Development Dept., ILO, Geneva
Massimo DE FRANCHI	Rural Employment (Regional), ILO Jobs and Skills Programme for Africa (JASPA)
Jasleen DHAMIJA	ILO Regional Office for Africa, PO Box 2788, Addis Ababa, Ethiopia
Bernard FOUNOU-TCHUIGOUA	Professeur, IDEP, Dakar, Sénégal
Venus B. KIMEI	Co-ordinator, Women Development, Women Development Section - Prime Ministers' Office, the United Republic of Tanzania

Simone LEROUX	Membre du Comité Exécutif de l'UGTCI, Union Générale des Travailleurs de Côte-d'Ivoire
Denia M. LEWILA	Personnel Officer Nchanga Consolidated Copper Mines Limited, Head Office, Box 30048, Lusaka, Zambia
Martha F. LOUTFI	Rural Employment Policies Branch, Employment and Development Dept., ILO, Geneva
Violet MATANHI	Director, Social Development and Communal Services, Ministry of Community Development and Women's Affairs, Earl Grey Building, Government of Zimbabwe, Salisbury, Zimbabwe
Aminata MBENGUE NDIAYE	Chef de la Division de la Promotion Humaine Secrétariat d'Etat à la Promotion Humaine, Sénégal
Marie-Hélène MOTTIN SYLLA	Chargée de Recherche et de Publication ENDA, Dakar, Sénégal
Bukola ONI	Head, Home Economics Division Federal Department of Rural Development Federal Ministry of Agriculture and Rural Development, Nigeria
M.D. RANDRIOMAMONJY	Home Economics Officer, FAO, Via delle Terme di Caracalla 00100, Rome, Italy
Cornelia RICHTER	Counsellor, Bundesministerium für Wirtschaftliche Zusammenarbeit, Bonn, Federal Republic of Germany
Marion ROOKHUIZEN	Ministry of Foreign Affairs, PO Box 20061, NL 2500 EB, The Hague, Netherlands
Marie-Angélique SAVANE	Présidente Association des Femmes Africaines pour la Recherche sur le Développement (AFARD/AAWORD), BP 3186, Dakar, Sénégal
Gloria SCOTT	Adviser on Women in Development, World Bank, 1818 H Street NW, Washington DC, 20433 USA
Aïssatou SOW BARRY	Conseiller Technique Secrétariat d'Etat à la Promotion Humaine, Sénégal

Yvette STEVENS

Technology and Employment Branch,
Employment and Development Dept.,
ILO, Geneva

Zenebeworke TADESSE

Department of Sociology, State
University of New York, Binghamton,
NY13901, USA

Awa THIONGANE

Chef de la Division des Synthèses
Economiques, Direction de la
Statistique du Sénegal, BP 116,
Dakar, Sénégal

Aminata TRAORE

Directrice des Etudes et Programme
Ministère de la Condition Féminine,
BP V200, Abidjan, Côte d'Ivoire

Kamoni TRAORE

Conseiller Régional en Education pour
le Développement Rural, BREDA,
UNESCO, Dakar , Sénégal

220